KT-442-676

Choosing Your Diploma

Jayne North

trotman t

LEICESTER LIBRARIES	
Askews	12-Jan-2011
	£12.99

Choosing Your Diploma

This first edition published in 2010 by Trotman Publishing, a division of Crimson Publishing Ltd, Westminster House, Kew Road, Richmond, Surrey TW9 2ND

©Trotman Publishing 2010

Author Jayne North

British Library Cataloguing in Publication Data
A catalogue record for this book is available from the British Library
ISBN 978 1 84455 203 0

All rights reserved. No part of this publication may be reproduced, stored in a retrieval system or transmitted in any form or by any means, electronic and mechanical, photocopying, recording or otherwise without prior permission of Trotman Publishing.

Typeset by RefineCatch Ltd, Bungay, Suffolk

Printed and bound in the UK by Ashford Colour Press, Gosport, Hants

Contents

PART THREE: END NOTE

About the author

Jayne North has 18 years' experience in careers education, information, advice and guidance and now works as an independent education consultant. Jayne has an in-depth knowledge of the 14–19 educational reforms and the new qualification framework as a result of working on 14–19 Workforce Support as the North West Information, Advice and Guidance (IAG) Champion for the Specialist Schools and Academies Trust (SSAT). She is also a qualified neurolinguistic Master Practitioner and coach and has developed many examples of good practice in establishing Guidance Network Partnerships, the 'Ready to Work' employability programme, S.T.E.P.S Community Volunteer Mentoring and motivational group work programme. Jayne is a successful bid writer and has contributed to the authoring and filming of many Careers Education Information, Advice and Guidance publications and resources on behalf of the Department for Children, Schools and Families (DCSF) and other organisations.

Introduction

What this book is about

Do you know what you want to do in the future? What job or career are you interested in? You might already have some ideas, or maybe not – this is fine either way.

Today there are more opportunities for young people than ever before, and during the next few years you will face some important decisions. This book is designed to help you explore one of the new opportunities available to you; an exciting qualification called the **Diploma**.

Choosing what to study represents a big decision and can feel a bit scary. The good news is that there is lots of help and advice available and you will be able to get plenty of support to help you make the decision that's right for you.

Enjoy reading this book to find out all you need to know about Diplomas and to help you make a well thought-out decision you are happy with.

How to use this book

Part 1 of the book looks at what Diplomas are and why they were introduced. It also explores why the qualification is different and why it might be the right option for you.

Part 2 is a directory of Diploma courses that looks at the range of subjects you can take.

Part 3 looks at what a Diploma could lead to and will signpost useful contacts and sources of support.

There may be terms and words in this book that you are unfamiliar with – to help with this there is a glossary of terms and initialisations included on p157. The first mention of each glossary term or initialisation in the text is highlighted in bold.

Please read this book in the way that suits you best. You may decide to look up a particular Diploma subject and go straight to that page, or you may decide to find out a bit more about Diplomas in general before looking at the range of subjects available. You can approach this book in whichever way you prefer. Table 1 will also help to point you in the right direction.

Table 1
Where to look in *Choosing Your Diploma*

Issue	Which section of the book?
I don't know very much about Diplomas	Part One, Chapter One
I would like to know what I could do after my Diploma course	Part Three
I know what subject area I am interested in and want to know more about the Diploma in this area	Part Two, Directory of subjects
I don't understand the levels of Diplomas available	Part One, Chapter One, Table 2
I would like to know where to get more information about Diplomas	Part Two, Directory of subjects Part Three, Sources of further information
I would like to take other qualifications alongside my Diploma. Can I?	Part Two, Directory of subjects – see Additional Specialist Learning under each line of learning
I am not sure I am suited to Diploma learning. How can I find out?	Chapter Two, Getting to Know Yourself quiz
How prepared are you to make your decisions about your future?	Part Three, Diploma Bingo

PART ONE

OPTIONS AND DECISIONS

CHAPTER ONE

Choosing the right options

Are you feeling excited? Puzzled? Worried? It's normal to feel this way when faced with big decisions and lots of different opportunities. Don't panic! This is your chance to take control of your learning and your education.

Choosing the right course may be one of the first big decisions you have to make. It is important to get as much information as possible to help you in making your decision. You can do this in many different ways, and reading this book is one of them.

Decision making should be challenging and exciting – it is your opportunity to take control of your education and shape your future! It is also your chance to start planning ahead for what you want to do next.

Remember – you are not alone in making these decisions. Everyone has to choose their options and goes through the same process. And don't forget, everyone needs a bit of help with decision making. Your choices are too important to leave to chance, so make sure that you get all the help and support you need to make the choice that is right for you.

What is a Diploma?

You may already be familiar with traditional qualifications like GCSEs and **A levels**, which are usually chosen and studied at 14 years and 16 years respectively. The Diplomas are new qualifications that are also available to the 14–19 age group and can be studied alongside GCSEs and A levels, letting you get the best of both worlds!

The Diplomas are different because they have been developed by employers, schools, colleges and universities with the aim of enabling young people to gain knowledge and develop their skills in a real-world environment and prepare themselves for the next stage in their learning or career pathway.

With a Diploma course you'll learn in a fun, hands-on style, both in and out of the classroom, and take on challenging projects.

Through studying a Diploma, you will develop a deeper knowledge of your main subject area, such as Sport and Active Leisure or Creative and Media, plus you will be able to broaden your study with other courses – these can be related to your main subject area, to your future ambitions to study at university or to a career you may be interested in. They could also be related to another interest or hobby you may have, for example computers, music or languages.

> # Jargon Buster: Applied Learning
>
> !
>
> Applied learning will allow you to put into action, in a work context, the theory that you're learning. This is different to vocational learning, which is designed to equip people with the knowledge, skills and competence required to work effectively in that sector.
>
> Diplomas are intentionally not 'occupational' qualifications; they are dual purpose, being designed to provide both academic and vocational pathways.

The Diploma includes applied learning and will help you develop work-relevant **employability skills** and maths, English and ICT in a creative and enjoyable way. It will appeal to you if you like practical subjects, problem solving and applying what you learn to real-life situations.

It's important to remember that the Diploma does not replace GCSEs or A levels; for example, in Year 10 you could start GCSEs alongside the Diploma, and if you are 16 years old taking the Advanced Diploma you could start additional A levels as well.

One advantage to studying a Diploma is that it will not narrow down your options in the future; in fact, the Diploma courses are very broad and will give you the chance to find out a lot more about the subject area you are interested in.

Whether you've got a career in mind, hope to go to university or just want to see what's out there, the Diploma is the perfect way to explore your options. It's a new qualification for 14–19-year olds and offers a mix of classroom learning and hands-on experience – all designed to prepare you for wherever you want to go in life.

At this stage, you will probably have a lot of questions – so read on, as this book will help you to understand these new and exciting qualifications called Diplomas.

> # Jargon Buster: Key Stage 4
>
> !
>
> Key Stage 4 is the term used to describe Years 10 and 11 in secondary schools. Normally, this is when you prepare for examinations taken towards the end of Year 11. However, preparation for some exam courses now starts in Year 9, or possibly even earlier, and many younger students are following Key Stage 4 courses in one or more subjects, so we have chosen to refer to Key Stage 4 rather than ages 14–16 in this book.

Why is the Diploma being introduced?

The Diploma was introduced in 2008 and forms part of a bigger set of changes to education for students aged between 14 and 19. The purpose of these changes is to help young people choose a qualification that suits their interests and learning style. GCSEs and A levels are also being updated, and more **Apprenticeships** will be available as well.

Since September 2008, 14–19-year olds have been able to take the two-year Diploma in a range of subject areas to gain valuable practical and theoretical skills for entering the workplace.

The Diploma can be taken at three different levels (Foundation, Higher and Advanced) and will give you an insight into different careers in your chosen subject area rather than providing training for a specific job.

Where is the Diploma available?

The Diploma is a new qualification that schools, colleges, employers and universities helped to develop. Diplomas are being taught throughout England, but not all subjects are available in all areas.

To find out more about which Diplomas are available in your area, you could speak to your careers co-ordinator or Connexions personal adviser, or you could see whether there's a teacher in your school who has responsibility for Diplomas.

Another good source of information on Diplomas would be your local online 14–19 prospectus (visit www.direct.gov.uk/14-19prospectus if you need help finding this). Your local prospectus will tell you where and which Diploma courses are available in your area.

The qualification

You can take a Diploma at three levels:

1. Level 1: Foundation Diploma – equivalent to five GCSEs at grades D to G
2. Level 2: Higher Diploma – equivalent to seven GCSEs at grades A* to C
3. Level 3: Advanced Diploma – equivalent to three-and-a-half A levels. There's also a shorter Progression Diploma equivalent to two-and-a-half A levels. The Progression Diploma has no optional elements.

Table 2 shows you the different levels that can be studied, when you can study them and what they are equivalent to.

Jargon Buster: Sector

In relation to a Diploma, the term 'sector' refers to a specific area of work or industry, such as construction, sport or hair and beauty.

Table 2
Diploma levels and equivalents

LEVEL 1	Foundation Diploma	Can be studied in Years 10 and 11 or post-16	Equivalent to up to 5 GCSEs at grades D–G
LEVEL 2	Higher Diploma	Can be studied in Years 10 and 11 or post-16	Equivalent to up to 7 GCSEs at grades A*–C
LEVEL 3	Progression Diploma	Can be studied post-16	Equivalent to up to 2.5 A levels
	Advanced Diploma	Can be studied post-16	Equivalent to up to 3.5 A levels

The Progression and Advanced Diplomas

The main difference between the Progression Diploma and the Advanced Diploma is that Progression learners do not need to complete an additional and specialist learning (ASL) component.

The course

The Diploma has three component parts:

1. **principal learning** – learning about your Diploma subject
2. **generic learning** – the essential skills you need for everyday life
3. **additional and specialist learning** – a choice of other subjects to help you understand more about your Diploma subject or to fulfil a personal interest.

Let's have a look at these three component parts in more detail.

Principal learning

At the core of the Diploma is the principal learning and this relates to the subject area you are interested in (e.g. Construction and the Built Environment or Hair and Beauty). Through the principal learning you will develop an understanding and knowledge of the sector and gain sector-specific skills.

Generic learning

In a Diploma, generic learning helps you to develop and apply the skills and knowledge you need for whatever you want to do. At each Diploma level, generic learning includes the four components described below.

A project

The project is an exciting piece of work that gives you the opportunity to demonstrate all of the things you have learnt while on your Diploma course. It provides you with the opportunity to choose the topic for yourself, and you can be creative in how you present it; for example, you could make a short film, write a report or record a webcast etc.

Part of the Advanced and Progression Diplomas is the Extended Project. This is also an option for A level or **AS level** students. To gain the qualification you must:

- choose a project of personal interest to yourself and agree it with a teacher,
  show through the project that you can plan, deliver and present an extended piece of work at Level 3.

Functional Skills in English, maths and ICT

Functional skills (see p14) are integral to your Diploma course and are the practical skills of English, maths and ICT. When applied, these help you work effectively in life.

Personal, learning and thinking skills (PLTS)

These are life skills that will help you to be successful whatever you decide to do in the future. Through PLTS, you will develop skills in:

- independent inquiry
- creative thinking
- reflective learning
- team working
- self-management
- effective participation.

You might already have some of these skills – why not consider each in turn and try to think of an example to demonstrate it? If you struggle with one, then a Diploma will help you to develop that skill further!

Work experience

A minimum of 10 days' work experience will allow you to put your learning into context. It will give you the opportunity to learn about the workplace and develop transferable skills (see p13) and knowledge. Work experience will develop your understanding of enterprise as you gain knowledge of the world of work and what employers are looking for when they recruit. You could work with a small local employer, seeing how their business is organised and how one person does a variety of roles such as finance, human resources and marketing. Or you might have the opportunity to do work experience in a large company, and look at how the finance department or customer services teams do their jobs.

Additional and specialist learning (ASL)

The ASL element of a Diploma course is another opportunity to personalise your Diploma because it gives you the opportunity to study a topic of your choice in more detail, or alternatively choose something different that will broaden your experience. ASL can include GCSEs, A/AS levels and vocational qualifications such as BTEC awards, normally at the same level of your course. For example if you chose to study for an Advanced Diploma then you may take an additional A level. These qualifications could be in another language, a science subject, performing arts etc. or a course that is related to a hobby, such as music, dance or art.

ASL allows you to follow your interests or career goals and tailor your learning programme to meet your aspirations. There are a large number of possible qualifications that can be taken alongside your principal learning to fulfil the ASL requirements.

Additional specialist learning (ASL)

Your choice of additional and specialist learning is really important because it may open, or close, the opportunity to certain progression routes, to particular subjects or to Diploma lines of learning. Given the broad range of choices open to you, it is essential for you to get some high-quality, up-to-date and unbiased information, advice and guidance (IAG) to help you choose the right qualifications.

CHAPTER TWO

Choosing your Diploma

What Diplomas are available?

There are currently 14 Diploma subjects available:

- Business Administration and Finance
- Construction and the Built Environment
- Creative and Media
- Engineering
- Environmental and Land-based Studies
- Hair and Beauty Studies
- Hospitality
- Information Technology
- Manufacturing and Product Design
- Public Services
- Retail Business
- Society, Health and Development
- Sport and Active Leisure
- Travel and Tourism.

Why is the Diploma different?

The Diploma is different to what you're used to. It is designed to help you make decisions about your future while keeping all your options open, and you can use it as a stepping stone to higher education, training and employment.

It helps you to explore subject areas, broaden your knowledge of a sector and gain valuable work experience without having to commit to a career in that area. You will also develop a range of skills which are transferable to whatever you want to do in the future.

A new qualification

The new Diploma will be a great route into both further study (e.g. university) and/or work, and will be recognised as a direct equivalent of GCSEs and A levels.

Let's take a look at some of the main differences to how you may have studied before.

- The Diplomas have been designed to give you the opportunity to learn through both theory and practice and this will give you a great head start in whichever area of work you choose.
- Alongside learning the theory, you will get the opportunity to learn in the workplace, often applying your classroom learning in context.
- You may benefit from learning at other sites, for example at a local school or college.
- The development of independent research and study skills will support you with self-directed study, where you will get the chance to have more control over what you learn by choosing your own project and your additional specialist learning.
- Depending on your choice of Diploma, you could get the opportunity to do a show/performance, take part in a business enterprise, develop a networked PC system, build a wall etc.
- You will develop invaluable employability skills for work in any sector.
- The life skills you develop will be useful to you in a whole variety of situations at work, study, leisure and home.

It's important to choose options that will interest and motivate you and that are suited to how you learn best. Try the quiz in Table 3 – it will help you to decide whether a Diploma course might be the right choice for you. Tick one option for each question.

Table 3
'Getting to know yourself' quiz

	No	Not sure – possibly!	Yes
Do you want to keep your options for the future open?			
Do you like to meet new people?			
Are you self-motivated and keen to learn in different ways?			
Would you like to learn in new places?			
Do you like problem solving and project work?			
Is there an area of work or job sector you are interested in?			
Do you want to develop transferable skills that employers are looking for?			

Once you've finished, count up how many of each you have ticked and read the corresponding advice below.

- **Mostly 'No'** Stop and consider this option seriously – there may be aspects of Diploma courses that are not right for you, so it may be necessary to do more research.

- **Mostly 'Not sure – possibly!'** Get ready to do some research: a Diploma course may be right for you, but you will need to find out more before making your decision. There are aspects of Diploma courses that you like and some you are not sure about!
- **Mostly 'Yes'** Great! A Diploma course may be just right for you – you will need to do a little more research and find out more about Diplomas to confirm this. The more research and preparation you do – by reading this book for example, talking to friends and family, using the Internet etc. – the more informed choices you'll be able to make about your future.

CHAPTER THREE

Why choose a Diploma?

This chapter considers the benefits and potential disadvantages of studying a Diploma, looking at the sort of questions you should ask yourself before deciding to take this qualification. It acknowledges that the Diploma is not suited to everybody and highlights what you need to consider when deciding what sort of qualification to opt for.

What are the benefits of studying a Diploma?

- A key feature of the Diploma is that it has been designed by employers and universities to ensure that you develop the skills that are required in higher education and by employers.
- A Diploma provides you with both theory and practical learning, helping you to develop a broad range of skills and knowledge. Therefore, any route is possible when you finish – further study, an Apprenticeship or a job with training.
- A Diploma gives you the opportunity to study and relate what you are learning to real-world situations. You get to do lots of projects and then apply what you know to solve practical, work-related problems. These problem-solving skills, combined with the skills you develop from having to be organised to complete a task, are key employability skills.
- You will usually be based at your own school or college and you may also get the opportunity to do part of your learning in another school or college or with an employer in the workplace.
- A Diploma will help you make decisions about what you want to do in the future while still keeping your options open.
- You will also gain transferable skills that are valued by employers in industry.
- A Diploma is based around broad subject areas and includes project-based learning. It will also give you the opportunity to choose additional specialist learning options that reflect your interests, abilities, career ambitions and learning styles.

Jargon Buster: Transferable Skills

These are versatile skills – e.g. team working, effective communication, negotiation and problem solving – that you can apply in a number of different situations. Transferable skills are valued by employers in the workplace, so it is important that you can recognise and talk about them.

Are there any disadvantages in studying for a Diploma?

Even if you think you know what job or career you are interested in, it is important to research your interests so you are clear what qualifications you need and are sure they will offer you the most appropriate learning style for you. Diplomas are project-based and hands-on, and you need to be able to work both in teams and under your own initiative. Look again at how your results from the 'Getting to know yourself' quiz (on p10) fit with Diploma learning.

Some people think that Diplomas narrow down your options in the future, but this isn't true. Although a Diploma may be related to a particular sector of industry, it is still very broad and will not prevent you going into another sector if you have the right skills and qualifications.

Something else you need to consider is that a Diploma may involve learning away from your own school. How would you feel about travelling somewhere else? Studying for a Diploma may also involve learning with students from other schools – how would you feel about this? Would you see it as an opportunity to make new friends?

You can get further help and information about progression routes and learning styles from your school careers resource centre or library, or your local Connexions centre (your school will be able to tell you where this is).

Could I move from Diplomas to other qualifications?

The Diploma is designed to be flexible, letting you take whichever route you feel best suits you – whether that's college, university, training or employment. And a Diploma does not replace existing options, so you can also take it alongside familiar courses such as GCSEs and A levels.

All Diploma students must meet a good standard in English, maths and ICT. This means you'll gain experience using them in practical situations, and you will take a functional skills test to demonstrate your achievements.

Jargon Buster: Functional Skills

Functional skills involve the practical application of your English, maths and ICT learning. By demonstrating these skills, you will be able to prove to employers that you can work effectively and independently. Functional skills are relevant to, and will help you in, all aspects of life.

Where will I study my Diploma?

If the Diploma subject you want to study is available locally, you can learn in the classroom. You could also spend time at another school or college, though, and you'll get the chance to spend time with an employer doing work experience – which may mean more travel than you're probably used to at the moment. Your school or college will help you make travel arrangements.

How long does it take to do a Diploma?

Diplomas usually take two years if you study full time. If you are doing a Foundation or Higher Diploma when you are aged 16 or over, you should be able to complete it in less time.

Doing a SWOT analysis

A SWOT analysis should be the first stage of your planning: it stands for **strengths, weaknesses, opportunities and threats**. Strengths and weaknesses are aspects of yourself that may affect you, while opportunities and threats are the external factors that can have an influence. Consider whether a SWOT analysis could help you in your research on Diplomas by asking yourself the questions below.

Tip – when you do a SWOT analysis, try to be as specific, realistic and straightforward about your answers as possible!

Strengths

- What sort of things do you do well and might help you study for a Diploma?
- What do other people regard as your strengths?

Weaknesses

- What aspects could you improve before taking a Diploma?
- What might be weaknesses for you during study for a Diploma?

Opportunities

- How could you turn your strengths into opportunities for yourself?
- What kind of opportunities will a Diploma offer you?

Threats

- Could there be any disadvantages to taking a Diploma, and what would they be?
- Might a Diploma present any negative factors for you?

PART TWO

DIRECTORY OF DIPLOMA SUBJECTS

CHAPTER FOUR

Directory of Diplomas

The Diploma is available in 14 subject areas and at three different levels, Foundation, Higher and Advanced. This chapter will give more detailed information about each subject or line of learning at all three levels.

Every subject is covered in the following way:

- overview of the Diploma subject area
- in-depth exploration of the Diploma at Foundation, Higher and Advanced level
- identification of the themes covered in the Diploma
- topics covered under the principal learning at each level
- ASL opportunities
- what you can do and where you can go after your Diploma
- ideas for possible future higher education courses and careers
- what Diploma students have to say about their courses and why they chose them
- where to get further information and other sources of support.

THE DIPLOMA IN BUSINESS ADMINISTRATION AND FINANCE

The world of business administration and finance is stimulating and fast-paced. Business is the means by which wealth is created in society; our economic and social well-being depends on it and our public services are financed by its profits.

The Diploma in Business Administration and Finance is an exciting qualification introduced in September 2009 that represents a major innovation in teaching and learning. It has been designed to help you meet the challenges of the fast-changing economy, whichever sector or industry you choose to work in.

The Diploma combines theoretical and applied learning and covers three main themes:

- business enterprise
- business administration
- finance.

These are some of the things you might do on your course:

- learn about entrepreneurs
- understand what is involved in running your own business
- learn how to research and develop your ideas
- market and sell a product or service that you've created
- understand how change affects business
- research technology's effect on business
- develop an understanding of how businesses can be affected by the global economy
- get the skills you need to manage finances e.g. how to open a bank account and how to budget etc.

If you're doing a Higher or Advanced Diploma you will cover more areas, including communications, accounting, marketing and sales, customer service, preparing for work and many more.

The Diploma in Business Administration and Finance at Foundation level

The Foundation Diploma in Business Administration and Finance may be suitable if you are interested in business but are not yet ready for the demands of a Level 2 qualification. The Foundation Diploma will benefit you by providing an engaging programme offering clear routes of progression to a wide range of options at Level 2.

The Foundation Diploma lets you discover the wide variety of business issues that affect everyday life; it will give you the opportunity to experience the business administration and finance sectors, develop relevant skills and qualities and still enable you to keep your options open.

Principal learning themes

Principal learning focuses on developing the knowledge and skills most relevant for the Diploma in Business Administration and Finance. At Foundation level, it will provide you with a broad introduction to this sector through the three themes of business enterprise, business administration and finance.

Business enterprise
You will learn about:

- the range of services and products available in the business sector
- why it is important to be creative and come up with new ideas
- why businesses need to carry out market research and promotion.

You could show what you have learned by:

- identifying a new product and the range of ways it could be marketed to different groups of people – you could carry out your own market research to do this.

Business administration
You will learn about:

- how businesses administrate themselves.

You could show what you have learned by:

- researching the role of staff in a human resources department, and then role-play the different jobs and responsibilities as part of a team.

Finance
You will learn about:

- the concept of money and its functions
- the most common sources of financial advice
- personal budgeting and different types of bank accounts.

You could show what you have learned by:

- working out what your weekly expenses are, for example the cost of your housing and utility bills, food, transport, leisure etc. and then working out how much money you would need to earn if you were living independently and supporting yourself financially.

Principal learning topics

The principal learning is divided into seven main topics of study, as described below.

Business enterprise

This topic includes:

- the main types of products and services in the business administration and finance sectors
- how innovation and creativity can benefit business.

Business administration

This topic includes:

- how administration can support businesses
- the reasons why effective administration is important to a business.

Personal finance and financial services

This topic includes:

- the concept, purpose and sources of money
- balancing income and expenditure.

Team working

This topic includes:

- what a team is and why businesses use teams to achieve their goals
- the role of effective communication when working in teams.

Customer service

This topic includes:

- what customer satisfaction is and why it is important to a business
- the different types of customer.

Sales

This topic includes:

- why sales are important to organisations
- the role of the salesperson and how to sell effectively.

Preparing for work

This topic includes:

- identifying the skills and qualities needed for the workplace
- where to get information, advice and guidance (IAG) about employment opportunities in the business administration and finance sector.

The Diploma in Business Administration and Finance at Higher level

The Higher Diploma in Business Administration and Finance may be suitable if you are interested in business and ready to progress to a Level 2 course, and would benefit from an engaging programme that provides you with clear progression routes to a wide range of Level 3 options.

Principal learning themes

The Higher Diploma in Business Administration and Finance further develops the three themes of business enterprise, business administration and finance. It will enable you to extend and apply your learning with increasing confidence and independence, and in many different situations – for example, those outlined below.

Business enterprise

You will learn about:

- how entrepreneurs are creative and innovative
- how to set up and run a business
- how technology can support a business effectively.

You could show what you have learned by:

- identifying a gap in the market and coming up with an idea for a new product or service and then, through market research, writing an informed business plan.

Business administration

You will learn about:

- the importance of administration and administrative systems.

You could show what you have learned by:

- building on the development of an idea for a new business, product or service and then identifying the key documents you need to include and reference when writing your business plan.

Finance

You will learn about:

- financial services and products
- key roles in finance such as insurance, banking and accountancy
- sources of business finance
- business taxation.

You could show what you have learned by:

- building on your new business idea and business plan to work out a budget, record transactions, projected income and expenditure, calculate tax and write a financial report, which you could present to a bank when seeking financial support.

Principal learning topics

At Higher level, the principal learning is divided into 11 main topics as follows.

Business enterprise

This topic includes:

- why creativity is important in developing business ideas and entrepreneurship
- what makes a new product or service a good business opportunity.

Business communication

This topic includes:

- learning about effective business communication
- different types of business communication, both internal and external.

Business administration

This topic includes:

- business roles that require administrative skills
- different administrative processes used in business.

Personal finance and financial services

This topic includes:

- the concept, purpose and sources of money
- where and how to get financial advice.

Business finance and accounting

This topic includes:

- different roles in business finance and accounting
- the sources of business finance.

Marketing and sales

This topic includes:

- developing an understanding of what marketing is and why branding is important to the success of a business
- the two types of market research – primary and secondary.

Team working

This topic includes:

- why team working is important to business and the factors that contribute to effective team working
- the roles of managers and their responsibilities in business.

Customer service

This topic includes:

- why customers and customer satisfaction are important to a business
- the understanding of internal and external customers.

Corporate social responsibility
This topic includes:

- the responsibility of organisations to different groups, including employees and customers
- why businesses need to operate responsibly, taking into account environmental and sustainability issues.

Responding to change
This topic includes:

- the reasons why change occurs in the business environment
- how change can affect businesses and employees.

Success at work
This topic includes:

- learning about job descriptions, person specifications and how they are used
- the purpose, content and format of a **CV**, a covering letter and an application form.

The Diploma in Business Administration and Finance at Advanced level

The Advanced Diploma in Business Administration and Finance may be suitable if you are interested in the sector, and will give you the chance to develop to an advanced level the skills and knowledge needed for work, enterprise and life, and also help progression to further and higher study.

At Advanced level, the principal learning requires more in-depth investigation, analysis and application of business skills; you will develop confidence and independence in your study through a flexible programme that is tailored to your chosen area of interest.

Principal learning themes

The Advanced Diploma in Business Administration and Finance further develops the three themes of business enterprise, business administration and finance in a wide range of work contexts, as set out below.

Business enterprise
You will learn about:

- how businesses are structured
- the processes involved in planning, setting up, running and closing a business
- the role of the entrepreneur
- the importance of innovation and creativity in business.

You could show what you have learned by:

- developing an idea for a new product or service, preparing a business pitch and then presenting it to potential investors in a role-play.

Business administration
You will learn about:

- information management
- project and event management
- the health and safety regulatory framework and why it is important.

You could show what you have learned by:

- planning an event to launch your product or service, while considering the health and safety framework and carrying out appropriate risk assessments.

Finance
You will learn about:

- the purpose and principles of financial accounting, business finance and taxation
- the structure, interpretation and use of financial documents
- how different types of financial data are used.

You could show what you have learned by:

- drawing up a business plan that identifies the most appropriate sources of borrowing to expand your business.

Principal learning topics

There are 11 topics underpinning the principal learning at Advanced level, as follows.

Business enterprise
This topic includes:

- how businesses in the UK are affected by the global economy
- the external factors and different interest groups that have an impact on how organisations operate.

Business communication
This topic includes:

- study of the theories underpinning current communication practices in business
- how electronic communication affects businesses and individuals worldwide.

Business administration
This topic includes:

- learning about administrative processes and why they are so important in business
- how organisations use business information effectively.

Personal finance and financial services

This topic includes:

- the concept, purpose and sources of money
- why people's attitude and approaches to finance are affected by their ethical and cultural beliefs.

Business finance and accounting

This topic includes:

- the purpose of accounting and different roles in business finance and accounting
- the purpose and current rates of corporate taxes.

Marketing and sales

This topic includes:

- how to apply key marketing principles and concepts to benefit business
- how different marketing techniques are used to benefit business and increase the demand for goods and services.

Team working

This topic includes:

- the essential characteristics, roles and responsibilities of team members, as well as team dynamics and motivation and how this affects outputs
- how effective team outputs contribute to improved organisational performance.

Customer service

This topic includes:

- why customer satisfaction is integral to the success of a business
- how product/service knowledge and other factors can contribute to customer satisfaction.

Corporate social responsibility

This topic includes:

- why corporate social responsibility is an important and emotive issue
- the key ethical issues facing businesses in today's global economy and in the future.

Responding to change

This topic includes:

- the internal and external factors, including technology, that can drive change in business, and the main current theories of change
- the impact that change can have on the whole organisation and its departments, teams and individual employees.

People at work

This topic includes:

- where you can get information and advice about career opportunities in business
- recruitment and selection processes and how job descriptions, person specifications, CVs etc. are used.

ASL for the Diploma in Business Administration and Finance

At each level, you can develop your own interests in business administration and finance by choosing specialist courses that relate to subject interests and career ambitions. You could, for example, learn more about accountancy if you are interested in finance, or consider human resources modules if you're more interested in personnel. Studying a foreign language can also be useful in a sector with so many international opportunities.

Alternatively, if you are thinking of higher education, you could choose subjects that will help such as law or economics.

You could also broaden your study and opportunities by opting for a subject that reflects another of your interests and career ambitions such as humanities, or a creative subject such as music or art.

Given the importance of ASL and the broad range of choices open to you, it would be really useful to get impartial IAG from a teacher or tutor. Specialist advice and guidance may be needed to help you to choose the right qualifications, and your school or college will be able to provide access to a Connexions adviser or careers adviser.

The Diploma in Business Administration and Finance and where it could take you

A Diploma in Business Administration and Finance will give you a fully rounded education and the skills you need for either university or work, and is a first step towards a career in the sector.

The sector spans a huge range of professions and the scope of jobs available is vast. It includes:

- financial adviser
- human resources manager
- actuary
- stock market dealer
- customer service adviser
- tax officer
- entrepreneur
- business development manager.

It could also lead you to a university degree in:

- business administration
- sales and marketing
- management
- human resources
- financial services
- any one of the vast range of different business-related disciplines available in higher education.

While the Diploma in Business Administration and Finance will give you an insight into the industry and prepare you to progress in that sector, you will also have the opportunity to apply to colleges, universities and employers for a broad range of opportunities. As the Diploma lets you study a combination of subjects, you will acquire a wide range of knowledge and experience and develop transferable skills, so you'll be well equipped no matter what you choose to do.

What business administration and finance students have to say about their courses

'Working with other people in an adult environment is the best.'

'I enjoy getting the skills to succeed in business and learning how to communicate better.'

'There is more hands-on learning, it's not just theory-based and you get to go out to do things e.g. enterprise activities.'

'The team working is great, better than working on your own all of the time!'

Further information

To find out more about the Diploma in Business Administration and Finance, speak to your teacher or careers adviser.

You can also find out more about Diplomas on these websites:

- www.direct.gov.uk/diplomas
- www.connexions-direct.com
- www.baf-diploma.org

If you would like to find out where you can study for this Diploma in your area, visit http://yp.direct.gov.uk/14-19prospectus

If you would like more information about the business administration and finance sector, you could also refer to the following resources.

Title: Break into Biz
Overview: This is a section of the Council for Administration website with over 30 job profiles.
Website: www.breakinto.biz

Title: icould
Overview: 'Real career stories told by real people' – video clips of people talking about their career paths, which you can search using a variety of parameters such as age, education level etc.
Website: www.icould.com

Title: National Guidance Research Forum: Labour Market Industry (LMI) Future Trends
Overview: This website provides detailed information on different sectors, including financial services and public administration.
Website: www.guidance-research.org/future-trends

THE DIPLOMA IN CONSTRUCTION AND THE BUILT ENVIRONMENT

The Diploma in Construction and the Built Environment was introduced in September 2008 and combines theoretical and applied learning to support you in developing knowledge of the construction industry and the skills that the employers in this sector are seeking.

This industry includes a wide range of careers in the building sector covering architecture, structural steelwork, heating and ventilation, painting and decorating and surveying. The principal learning in the Diploma has three main themes:

- design the built environment
- create the built environment
- value and use the built environment.

The Diploma in Construction and the Built Environment at Foundation level

The Foundation Diploma in Construction and the Built Environment may be suitable if you are interested in the sector but not yet ready for the demands of a Level 2 qualification. It will benefit you by providing an interesting programme with clear routes of progression to a wide range of options at Level 2.

Through the principal learning element, the Foundation Diploma in Construction and the Built Environment will let you discover how construction technology is used and enable you to develop the transferable skills needed for the sector while still keeping your options open.

Principal learning themes

The principal learning in the Foundation Diploma will offer a broad introduction to the sector through the three themes of design, create, value and use.

Design the built environment
You will learn about:

- how the built environment affects people and communities.

You could show what you have learned by:

- carrying out a survey of proposed developments in your area to identify building trends.

Create the built environment
You will learn about:

- construction methods and techniques.

You could show what you have learned by:

- wiring an electrical circuit to power a light.

Value and use the built environment
You will learn about:

- maintaining buildings and structures.

You could show what you have learned by:

- surveying your own learning environment, identifying opportunities for improvement and writing an improvement plan.

Principal learning topics
There are seven topics underpinning the principal learning in the Foundation Diploma, and these are set out below.

Design the built environment: design influences
This topic includes:

- factors influencing the design process
- how planning contributes to the design process.

Design the built environment: apply design principles
This topic includes:

- how design principles are applied in practice and why a range of structures are designed in certain ways
- identifying the job opportunities in designing the built environment.

Create the built environment: using tools
This topic includes:

- how to safely use and maintain tools for practical craft activities
- use of appropriate hand tools and personal protective equipment to carry out simple practical craft activities.

Create the built environment: methods and materials
This topic includes:

- changes that have taken place in construction materials
- the influences of mechanisation and new materials on construction methods.

Value and use the built environment
This topic includes:

- the impact of the built environment
- the life-cycle of structures and their impact on economic and social development.

Maintenance of the built environment
This topic includes:

- the principles and practices of basic building maintenance
- how to carry out simple practical building maintenance in a safe and effective manner.

Modern methods of construction
This topic includes:

- how modern construction methods have an impact on traditional forms of construction
- learning about a range of modern construction techniques and the traditional methods that they have replaced.

The Diploma in Construction and the Built Environment at Higher level

The Higher Diploma in Construction and the Built Environment may be suitable if you are interested in this sector and ready to progress to a Level 2 course, and if you would benefit from an engaging programme with clear routes of progression to a wide range of options at Level 3.

Principal learning themes

The Higher Diploma in Construction and the Built Environment further develops the three themes of design, create and value and use the built environment. It will help you develop your confidence and be able to apply your learning in a wide range of work contexts, as described below.

Design the built environment
You will learn about:

- design considerations and architectural features associated with the built environment.

You could show what you have learned by:

- identifying an environmental design challenge and developing a design that takes account of environmental factors.

Create the built environment
You will learn about:

- the tools and practical techniques used in design and construction.

You could show what you have learned by:

- building a brick wall to demonstrate the use of coloured bricks as a design feature.

Value and use the built environment

You will learn about:

- the importance of managing built structures well.

You could show what you have learned by:

- researching the building maintenance department of your school or college and considering how they maintain the building to ensure everyone's health and safety.

Principal learning topics

There are seven topics underpinning the principal learning in the Higher Diploma, as outlined below.

Design the built environment: the design process

This topic includes:

- the factors that influence design, including the incorporation of utilities such as gas and water
- how utilities are accommodated in the design process.

Design the built environment: materials and structures

This topic includes:

- learning how different construction materials and common structural forms and building elements are used in design
- use of sustainable materials and how they influence the design process.

Design the built environment: applying design principles

This topic includes:

- applying design principles in a design project
- learning how different materials may be suitable for the same design.

Create the built environment: structures

This topic includes:

- a range of methods used in constructing substructure
- a range of methods used in constructing superstructure.

Create the built environment: using tools

This topic includes:

- careers and career pathways in the construction industry
- hazards and risks in relation to the construction of the built environment.

Value and use the built environment: communities

This topic includes:

- the way the built environment impacts on individuals and communities
- the residential, industrial and commercial property market.

Value and use the built environment: facilities management
This topic includes:

- the processes involved in preserving, maintaining and managing the built environment, and how this contributes to wealth creation and quality of life
- the way built structures are operated, including relevant health and safety legislation.

The Diploma in Construction and the Built Environment at Advanced level

The Advanced Diploma in Construction and the Built Environment is suitable if you are interested in the sector, and will help you develop to an advanced level the skills and knowledge needed both in the workplace and everyday life. It should help progression to further and higher study as well.

If you are ready to take a Level 3 qualification, it will provide you with a combination of applied and theoretical learning. If you have an interest in this diverse sector, the Advanced Diploma will help you to develop the understanding, knowledge and skills needed for the sector and to go on to further and higher study, while letting you keep your options open.

Principal learning themes

The principal learning that underpins the Advanced Diploma in Construction and the Built Environment offers valuable experience of the industry and develops the three themes of design, create, value and use the built environment as follows.

Design the built environment
You will develop an understanding of:

- the extent and significance of the built environment and what shapes, develops and influences it.

You could show what you have learned by:

- identifying a design challenge and producing a report that includes a design proposal and strategies to protect and maintain the environment.

Create the built environment
You will develop an understanding of:

- the construction and built environment industries.

You could show what you have learned by:

- arranging a construction careers fair for younger pupils and inviting local architects, building managers, quantity surveyors, local authority building services etc. to exhibit and deliver presentations.

Value and use the built environment
You will learn about:

- how site developments affect the communities that use them.

You could show what you have learned by:

- identifying a local development and carrying out a survey to canvass public opinion about the project.

Principal learning topics

There are seven topics underpinning the principal learning in the Advanced Diploma, which are as follows.

Design the built environment: the design factors
This topic includes:

- the impact of a wide range of factors considered in designing the built environment
- how changing styles, approaches to design, political policies and funding, including the cyclical nature of growth and recession, have an effect on the design process.

Design the built environment: stages in the design and planning process
This topic includes:

- the skills needed to explore urban design and its influence on the urban environment
- learning about the different stages of the design and planning processes.

Design and the built environment: physical and environmental influences
This topic includes:

- health, safety and environmental factors that influence the design of the built environment
- learning about the provision of primary services utilities such as gas and electricity, and assessing the impact of climate change on design.

Create the built environment: health, safety and environmental issues
This topic includes:

- how to protect and maintain the environment during construction
- health, safety and environmental factors.

Create the built environment: management processes
This topic includes:

- an understanding of the construction processes required to create substructures (such as the foundations for a building) and superstructures (the part of the building above the ground)
- management of projects, including quality assurance and monitoring.

Value and use the built environment: adding value to the wider community
This topic includes:

- engaging stakeholders and communities in the development and use of the built environment
- the social, economic and commercial contribution to the wider community.

Value and use the built environment: protecting and maintaining
This topic includes:

- how to protect and maintain the environment
- how to minimise environmental impact through the use of buildings and structures.

ASL for the Diploma in Construction and the Built Environment

At each level of the Diploma, you can develop your own interests in construction and the built environment by choosing specialist courses that relate to your subject interests and career ambitions. You could, for example, earn more about environmental housing or building regulations; you might instead choose to develop your practical skills in bricklaying or joinery. Alternatively, if you are thinking of going to university you could choose subjects that will help, such as maths or ICT.

You could also broaden your study and later opportunities by opting for a subject that reflects another of your interests or career ambitions, e.g. a science, a language or a creative subject.

Given the importance of ASL and the broad range of choices open to you, it would be really useful to get impartial information, advice and guidance from a teacher or tutor. Specialist advice and guidance may be needed to help you to choose the right qualifications and your school or college will be able to provide access to a Connexions adviser or careers adviser.

The Diploma in Construction and the Built Environment and where it could take you

In addition to giving you a head start in the sector, a Diploma in Construction and the Built Environment will help you to develop the skills and knowledge you will need for employment or further study, including university.

The construction and the built environment sector spans a huge range of professions and the scope of jobs available is vast. It includes:

- building services engineer
- quantity surveyor
- bricklayer
- civil engineer

- joiner
- stonemason
- facilities management
- construction manager
- architect.

The Advanced Diploma could lead you to a university degree in construction management, building services management planning or architecture. However, it is always advisable to contact university admissions tutors to check whether the Diploma is a suitable route into the course that interests you and whether any particular ASL is required.

Nevertheless, the Diploma in Construction and the Built Environment teaches a combination of subjects and allows you to develop transferable skills so it will be useful whatever you choose to do.

What construction and the built environment students have to say about their courses

---

'It is harder than I thought it would be, but I am still enjoying it – every day is different.'

'I like my Diploma because I get to work with people from other schools.'

'The work doesn't always feel like work, it's just good to do a mix of different things.'

Further information

To find out more about the Diploma in Construction and the Built Environment, speak to your teacher or careers adviser.

You can also find more information about Diplomas on these websites:

- www.direct.gov.uk/diplomas
- www.connexions-direct.com
- www.cbediploma.co.uk

If you'd like to find out where you can study for this Diploma in your area, you can visit http://yp.direct.gov.uk/14-19prospectus

If you would like more information about the construction and built environment sector you could refer to the following resources.

Title: Construction Skills
Overview: Click the 'Working in construction' tab on the home page for careers information for young people.
Website: www.cskills.org

Title: The Sector Skills Council for Building Services Engineering
Overview: Click 'Careers' on the home page to access the 'Good Day for your Career' website and careers/labour market industry updates. Click 'Qualifications and Apprenticeships' for information about 14–19 Diplomas, Apprenticeships and Foundation Degrees.
Website: www.summitskills.org.uk

Title: bconstructive
Overview: The bconstructive website has information for people of all ages. Look at the links under 'Careers' on the home page to see case studies, find out about Apprenticeships and choose a construction career with the help of a virtual careers adviser.
Website: www.bconstructive.co.uk

Title: Careersbox
Overview: Careersbox is a free online careers film library. Type 'construction' in the search box and press 'enter' to view the case studies.
Website: www.careersbox.co.uk

Title: Construction Youth Trust
Overview: The Trust helps young people facing financial barriers, lack of aspiration, poor understanding of the construction and built environment sector and gender or ethnicity barriers. Its programmes range from individual bursaries to construction skills courses and from work placement schemes to guidance sessions.
Website: www.constructionyouth.org.uk

Title: Commission for Architecture and the Built Environment (CABE) – careers section
Overview: Young people can browse CABE profiles and case studies to find what sort of built environment career might suit them.
Website: www.cabe.org.uk/education/careers

THE DIPLOMA IN CREATIVE AND MEDIA

The Diploma in Creative and Media was introduced in September 2008, and lets you learn through a combination of theoretical and applied learning, developing your knowledge, understanding and skills in a variety of different contexts. It also gives you the opportunity to learn how to think and work creatively and see a project through from start to finish. The Diploma in Creative and Media allows you to progress into further and higher education, training or employment both in and outside the creative and media industries.

The Diploma in Creative and Media will help you gain knowledge of the creative industries, including film, dance, publishing, drama and fashion. You will develop invaluable transferable skills that will improve your employment opportunities in or outside of the sector.

The principal learning underpinning the Diploma in Creative and Media covers four main themes and will provide you with the industry-specific skills and knowledge you will need.

- creativity in context – exploration of what can influence the creative process; for example, the environment, change, society and culture
- thinking and working creatively – how to explore creative processes and the development of relevant skills and techniques
- principles, processes and practice – practical application of skills and techniques to turn your creative ideas into reality
- creative businesses and enterprise – awareness of the creative industries, and the skills and qualities required in the sector.

Application of these themes are covered in more than 20 sector-related disciplines and these will be updated to meet the changing needs of the industries. Currently, the disciplines are:

- 2D visual art
- 3D visual art
- craft
- graphic design
- product design
- fashion
- textiles
- footwear
- advertising
- drama
- dance

- music
- film
- television
- audio and radio
- interactive media
- publishing
- animation
- computer games
- photo imaging
- creative writing.

The Diploma in Creative and Media at Foundation level

The Foundation Diploma in Creative and Media may be suitable if you are not yet ready for the demands of Level 2 learning, but would benefit from an engaging programme that provides clear routes of progression to a wide range of options at that level.

The Foundation Diploma presents a new opportunity to learn about the growing creative and media industries, combining theoretical and applied learning to support you in developing a broad base of skills and knowledge.

Principal learning themes

The principal learning in the Foundation Diploma in Creative and Media covers four main themes, as set out below.

Creativity in context
You will learn about:

- developing creative ideas and ways of working.

You could show what you have learned by:

- making a webcast working in a small team, each of you taking on a different responsibility – script writing, production, direction, editing etc.

Thinking and working creatively
You will learn about:

- devising ideas in response to a brief and collaborating to develop ideas.

You could show what you have learned by:

- planning the launch of a new product including designing the logo, marketing and public relation materials and writing a pitch.

Principles, processes and practice
You will learn about:

- the key stages in the creative process and become familiar with the practices involved at each stage.

You could show what you have learned by:

- planning the launch of a new product, researching which materials and technologies to use and how to employ them to maximum effect.

Creative businesses and enterprise
You will learn about:

- the creative and media sectors, what it is really like to work in the industry and the importance of self-development to support progression.

You could show what you have learned by:

- presenting the pitch for a new product to a panel and filming the meeting to support reflection and learning.

You will get the opportunity to apply your learning in an area of interest to you, possibly in one of the creative and media sectors, or in a virtual creative and media environment in your own or another school or college.

You must demonstrate learning in a minimum of six different disciplines across the whole of your programme of study on the Foundation Diploma. There are currently over 20 disciplines available, as listed on p40.

The Diploma in Creative and Media at Higher level

The Higher Diploma in Creative and Media gives you the chance to explore a range of practical skills in the sector while developing broad knowledge to underpin them. It is a new qualification offering first-hand experience of this exciting industry.

The Higher Diploma in Creative and Media may be suitable if you are ready to proceed to Level 2 learning.

Principal learning themes

The Higher Diploma in Creative and Media lets you develop further the four principal themes of creativity in context, thinking and working creatively, principles, process and practice and creative businesses and enterprise in the ways explained below.

Creativity in context

You will learn about:

- a diverse range of cultures and the historical development of products and practices.

You could show what you have learned by:

- identifying a product that has been used over the years and research how it has developed historically e.g. ethically, product design, content, advertising and marketing.

Thinking and working creatively

You will learn about:

- developing ideas and how to think creatively and with increasing confidence.

You could show what you have learned by:

- experimenting with different ideas in performance and using a range of different methods and equipment.

Principles, processes and practice

You will learn about:

- production processes and using a broader range of materials and equipment.

You could show what you have learned by:

- using new technologies to design and create a product or piece of music.

Creative businesses and enterprise

You will learn about:

- what the creative and media sector is really like, what employment opportunities there are and routes for career progression.

You could show what you have learned by:

- researching the changes in a sector of the creative and media industry through history.

At Higher level, the principal learning will give you the opportunity to experience the breadth of this sector, with more than half of your applied learning having to be in context. The units offer the opportunity for project-led work, and you will be able to develop your skills further across a broad range of creative and media disciplines. You should also begin to develop your critical thinking and analytical skills.

At Higher level, the project-based work supports you in developing your confidence and becoming more independent and you will be able to progress your own ideas creatively.

The Diploma in Creative and Media at Advanced level

The Advanced Diploma in Creative and Media may be suitable if you are ready to take a Level 3 qualification. Its blend of applied and theoretical learning will engage you if you are interested in exploring the creative and media sector while remaining in full-time education.

The Advanced Diploma will give you a qualification that lets you go on to higher education, employment, Apprenticeships or Level 4 qualifications, while developing your understanding of the sector and enhancing your skills.

Principal learning themes

The Advanced Diploma in Creative and Media will help you take the four principal themes outlined above to a new level.

Creativity in context

You will learn about:

- the diverse range of creative and media products and critical appraisal of the work and techniques of a wide range of practitioners

- how the historical development of principles and practices can influence contemporary practice.

You could show what you have learned by:

- researching and presenting a study of fashion through the ages
- investigating how photography has changed with technological advances.

Thinking and working creatively
You will learn about:

- how to take a more critical perspective in developing ideas and analysing those of others.

You could show what you have learned by:

- responding to an interior design brief from a client by researching paint, colour, paper and furnishings and preparing a mood board for presentation.

Principles, processes and practice
You will learn about:

- developing the basic skills and techniques explored at Higher level and using creativity, imagination and innovation in their application.

You could show what you have learned by:

- responding to an advertising brief by researching the different methods available appropriate to the potential customer base.

Creative businesses and enterprise
You will learn about:

- the key knowledge and skills that will support future employment or self-employment in the creative and media industries or in other unrelated industries.

You could show what you have learned by:

- investigating employment opportunities in the sector and identifying employment trends by speaking to professionals across a range of creative and media disciplines, or researching global and environmental changes and how these will affect the sector.

ASL for the Diploma in Creative and Media

At each level, you can develop your own interests in creative and media by choosing specialist courses that relate to your subject interests and career ambitions. You could, for example, learn more about photography through the ages, media influences or sound technology. Alternatively, if you are thinking of going to university, you could choose subjects that will help your application such as A levels in English or History.

You could also broaden your study and opportunities by opting for a subject that reflects another of your interests or career ambitions, such as a science, a language or a humanities subject.

Given the importance of ASL and the broad range of choices open to you it would be really useful to get impartial information, advice and guidance from a teacher or tutor. Specialist advice and guidance may be needed to help you choose the right qualifications and your school or college will be able to provide access to a Connexions adviser or careers adviser.

The Diploma in Creative and Media and where it could take you

The creative and media sector is diverse and fast-growing, with a strong reputation for quality and innovation. Many in the sector are self-employed, and freelancers account for 40% of the workforce.

A Diploma in Creative and Media will give you the skills you need for an industry that is changing rapidly thanks to technological advances. The Diploma will also support you in applying for further study, university, training or work.

The creative and media sector spans a huge range of professions and the scope of jobs available is very wide. It includes:

- special effects technician
- costume designer
- sound technician
- publication editor
- media researcher
- film and digital image maker
- graphic designer
- fashion designer
- computer games designer.

It could lead you to a university degree in any number of subjects, including animation, textiles, dance or film, or equally languages, philosophy, politics or architecture.

While the Diploma in Creative and Media will provide an insight into the broad range of opportunities in the sector and prepare you to progress in that sector, you will also be able to keep your options open and apply to colleges, universities and employers. As the Diploma allows you to study a combination of subjects, acquire a wide range of knowledge and experience and develop transferable skills, you will be well equipped no matter what you choose to do.

What creative and media students have to say about their courses

---

'I was a bit nervous starting my course because none of my friends were doing a Diploma. But it was the right move – I love it and I have made lots of new friends too.'

'The Diploma has given me the chance to try things I wouldn't have done otherwise. Last week I visited a local TV studio to look at the jobs behind the scenes – it was really interesting!'

Further information

To find out more about the Diploma in Creative and Media, speak to your teacher or careers adviser.

You can also find more information about Diplomas online at:

* www.direct.gov.uk/diplomas
* www.connexions-direct.com

If you'd like to find out where you can study for this Diploma in your area, you can visit http://yp.direct.gov.uk/14-19prospectus

If you would like more information about the creative and media sector, you could refer to the following resources:

Title: Introduction to Project and Production Schedule
Overview: This offers an overview of project and production schedules, explaining what a producer does and offering a budgeting exercise, marketing exercise and a technical theatre task for students.
Website: www.glyndebourne.com/education/resource/creative_and_media_diploma_resources/

Title: Creative Choices: Essential kit throughout your career
Overview: This website looks at a broad area of the sector, including advertising, design and music.
Website: www.creative-choices.co.uk

Title: Skillset
Overview: Skillset is the industry body that supports skills and training in the UK's creative industries
Website: www.skillset.org

THE DIPLOMA IN ENGINEERING

The Diploma in Engineering was introduced in September 2008 to build on the rich history of engineering in the UK and ensure that the next generation of engineers have the right skills.

The Diploma will enable you to learn via a combination of theoretical and applied learning, developing your knowledge, understanding and skills in a variety of different contexts. You will get the opportunity to use your maths, science, technology and creative skills to design and make products. The Diploma in Engineering allows you to progress into further and higher education, into training or into employment both in and outside of the engineering sector.

The principal learning underpinning the Diploma in Engineering will provide you with the industry-specific skills and knowledge you will need, with at least half the principal learning in an engineering environment and involving engineering activities. You will get the chance to experience and engage with real-world engineering activities and work with people from an engineering background.

The principal learning element is underpinned by three themes:

- basic engineering principles
- the importance and impact of engineering on our lives
- what makes innovations succeed, how new materials contribute to design, and how to develop and launch new ideas.

The Diploma in Engineering at Foundation level

The Foundation Diploma offers a new route into the engineering sector if you are at Level 1. The Foundation Diploma in Engineering may be suitable if you don't yet feel ready for the demands of a Level 2 course but would do well with an engaging programme that gives clear progression to a wide range of options at Level 2.

The principal learning component of the Foundation Diploma in Engineering will provide you with a broad base of skills relevant to the world of engineering and its current and future impact on society and the economy.

Principal learning themes

Three themes underpin the principal learning in the Foundation Diploma.

The engineered world
You will learn about:

- how engineering has shaped the world we live in.

You could show what you have learned by:

- researching how technological advances have influenced engineering.

Discovering engineering technology
You will learn about:

- how to produce simple engineering drawings and diagrams.

You could show what you have learned by:

- using software to design a multifunctional children's toy.

Engineering the future
You will learn about:

- the impact of recycling.

You could show what you have learned by:

- researching an ethical company and how through recycling it manufactures its product.

Principal learning topics

Principal learning in the Foundation Diploma in Engineering consists of seven topics.

Introducing the world of engineering
This topic includes:

- the sectors of engineering and the types of jobs available in the industry
- the contribution engineering makes to the social and economic development of the world we live in.

Practical engineering and communication skills
This topic includes:

- health and safety issues
- the cutting, forming and joining processes used in manufacturing engineered products.

Using computer-aided engineering
This topic includes:

- how software packages are used to design products
- how product design and manufacture relates to computer-aided engineering.

Routine maintenance operations
This topic includes:

- the types of maintenance procedures carried out in industry
- the documentation used when planning and maintaining engineered products and services.

Introduction to engineering materials
This topic includes:

- the types of material that engineers use
- the basic properties of engineering materials.

Introduction to electronics
This topic includes:

- standard symbols used to represent electronic components
- planning the construction of electronic circuits.

Engineering the future
This topic includes:

- developments in materials and engineering technology that affect everyday life
- renewable energy sources and environmental issues.

The Diploma in Engineering at Higher level

The Higher Diploma in Engineering is designed to introduce you to the skills and knowledge that you need to succeed in today's workplace. It combines theoretical and applied learning to offer an exciting, relevant insight into the engineering sector.

The Higher Diploma in Engineering may be suitable if you are ready to access Level 2 learning.

Principal learning themes

Three themes underpin the principal learning in the Higher Diploma, as follows.

The engineered world
You will learn about:

- the different engineering sectors and engineering's diverse roles.

You could show what you have learned by:

- researching the range of employment opportunities in engineering and the professional bodies and organisations that support them.

Discovering engineering technology
You will learn about:

- using software packages and computer systems to design and manufacture engineering parts.

You could show what you have learned by:

- using software to design an engineering solution.

Engineering the future
You will learn about:

- the relationship between innovative engineering design and business success.

You could show what you have learned by:

- researching how to patent engineering designs.

Principal learning topics

The principal learning for the Higher Diploma in Engineering covers the eight topics described below.

The engineered world
This topic includes:

- the engineering sectors and their products and services
- jobs and career paths in engineering and the role of the professional bodies.

Engineering design
This topic includes:

- the importance of an engineering product's performance and functions
- key requirements of design briefs.

Engineering applications of computers
This topic includes:

- the use of computers in process control and manufacturing
- the use of microprocessor controllers in domestic products.

Producing engineering solutions
This topic includes:

- properties of materials
- health and safety and standards.

Constructing electronic and electrical systems
This topic includes:

- basic electrical and electronic principles
- testing and fault finding.

Manufacturing engineering
This topic includes:

- performing quality checks
- the use of computer-controlled machines.

Maintenance

This topic includes:

- different types of maintenance processes
- interpreting manufacturers' information and data sheets.

Innovation, enterprise and technological advance

This topic includes:

- how innovation and creativity benefit engineering
- the role of research and development in designing and developing products.

The Diploma in Engineering at Advanced level

The Advanced Diploma in Engineering may be suitable if you are ready to take a Level 3 qualification. It combines applied and theoretical learning, which will appeal to you if you are interested in exploring the engineering sector while remaining in full-time education.

Principal learning themes

Four themes underpin principal learning in the Advanced Diploma and are detailed below.

The engineered world

You will learn about:

- engineering businesses, their processes and the internal and external factors that affect the business.

You could show what you have learned by:

- working to a client's brief to design a multifunctional kitchen utensil and demonstrating how research, project management, design, production and marketing contribute to engineering success.

Discovering engineering technology

You will learn about:

- applying the use of computer-aided design (CAD) in a range of engineering contexts.

You could show what you have learned by:

- using CAD to produce a 3D model of a multifunctional kitchen utensil.

Engineering the future

You will learn about:

- how to use maths and science in engineering analysis, design and problem solving.

You could show what you have learned by:

- applying mathematical or scientific principles to the design process for an engineered product, for example the production of solar covers for swimming pools.

Analytical methods for engineering
You will learn about:

- the knowledge, skills and understanding of maths and science that engineers need in analysis, design and problem solving.

You could show what you have learned by:

- using mathematical or scientific problem-solving skills in research and analysis to support the design of a flexible solar cover for a swimming pool.

Principal learning topics
The following ten topics are covered in the principal learning for the Advanced Diploma in Engineering.

Engineering businesses and career pathways
This topic includes:

- how engineering businesses are influenced by internal and external factors
- legislation in engineering businesses.

Engineering and the environment
This topic includes:

- the problem of resource depletion
- pollution control, preventing both air and water contamination.

Applications of CAD
This topic includes:

- the use of 2D and 3D software
- drawing to industrial standards.

Selection and application of engineering materials
This topic includes:

- destructive and non-destructive testing methods
- effects of processing on the structure and behaviour of materials.

Instrumentation and control engineering
This topic includes:

- signals and wave guides
- open-loop, closed-loop, feed-forward and feedback control theory.

Maintaining engineering systems and products
This topic includes:

- effective maintenance strategies
- closed-loop engineering systems.

Production and manufacturing
This topic includes:

- different types of manufacturing processes
- computer-aided engineering, computer-aided manufacturing and computer numerical control.

Innovative design and enterprise
This topic includes:

- innovative engineering designs and new technologies
- designing for the environment.

Mathematical techniques and applications for engineers
This topic includes:

- trigonometric identities and equations for statics and dynamics, electrical laws, power factor correction, signals and phasors
- algebra, quadratic equations, indices, binomial expansion and partial fractions.

Scientific principles and applications for engineers
This topic includes:

- electrical properties of solids, resistance and resistivity, dielectric constants and capacitance
- thermodynamics, expansion and compression of gases, heat of combustion.

ASL for the Diploma in Engineering

At each level, you can choose specialist courses that relate to your own interests in Engineering as well as to any of your future career ideas. You could, for example, learn more about medical engineering, aeronautical engineering or robotics. If you are going to go to university, you could choose subjects that will help, such as A level Maths or Physics.

You could also broaden your study and opportunities by opting for a subject that reflects another of your interests and career ambitions, e.g. a science, a language or a humanities subject.

Did you know?

If you want to carry on studying engineering at university, it would be a good idea to take the 'maths for engineers' option as part of the Advanced Diploma in Engineering.

Given the importance of ASL and the broad range of choices open to you it would be really useful to get impartial information, advice and guidance from a teacher or tutor. Specialist advice and guidance may be needed to help you to choose the right qualifications, and your school or college will be able to provide access to a Connexions adviser or careers adviser.

The Diploma in Engineering and where it could take you

A Diploma in Engineering will give you the skills you need for either university or work, and is a first step towards a career in the sector.

The engineering sector spans a huge range of professions – the range of jobs available is vast and includes:

- aerospace engineer
- gas network engineer
- motor vehicle technician
- mechanical engineer
- marine engineer
- chemical engineer
- refrigeration engineer.

After studying the Diploma in Engineering, you can go on to study at degree level in one of the following subjects: aeronautical engineering, automotive engineering, biomedical materials science, building services engineering, electrical and electronic engineering or mechanical engineering.

You are not limited to working in the engineering sector with this Diploma because Diplomas are designed to teach a combination of subjects as well as transferable skills and a range of knowledge; these are all needed by colleges, universities and employers.

What engineering students have to say about their courses

'It's great being a test pilot for a new qualification. I was interested in mechanical engineering now I would like to try aeronautical engineering.'

'I chose the Advanced Diploma because I wanted to go to university to study Engineering but was unsure about what type of engineering. This is helping me to make up my mind!'

'I have made some great new friends who I wouldn't have met if I hadn't chosen my Diploma course.'

Further information

To find out more about the Diploma in Engineering, speak to your teacher or careers adviser.

You can also find more information about the Diploma on these websites:

- www.direct.gov.uk/diplomas
- www.connexions-direct.com
- www.engineeringdiploma.com

If you'd like to find out where you can study for this Diploma in your area, go to http://yp.direct.gov.uk/14-19prospectus

If you would like more information about the engineering sector, you could refer to the following resources as well.

Title: British Aerospace (BAE) Systems Education Programme
Overview: This site is designed to inspire you to take up science and engineering.
Website: www.baesystemseducationprogramme.com

Title: Cogent: Skills for Science-Based Industries
Overview: The industries covered by this sector skills council include chemicals, pharmaceuticals, oil, gas, nuclear, petroleum and polymers. The site profiles these and their training and learning opportunities, including Apprenticeships. There is a page about careers outlining a huge range of pathways – job descriptions, key processes, entry level, industry standards, competencies, required knowledge and pay and conditions.
Website: www.cogent-ssc.com

Title: Enginuity
Overview: This site offers free, downloadable engineering and technology careers resources.
Website: www.enginuity.org.uk

Title: Future Morph
Overview: This online resource highlights jobs that studying science, technology, engineering and mathematics subjects can lead to. It offers games, activities, information and case studies to help young people explore opportunities, become more aware of their own abilities and interests and plan their next steps in learning or work.
Website: www.futuremorph.org

Title: Scenta
Overview: Set up by the Engineering and Technology Board (ETB), this site provides a gateway to the best information and resources for those pursuing a career in science, engineering and technology. It also allows you to search for engineering role models and inspirational projects and articles.
Website: www.scenta.co.uk

Title: Semta
Overview: The Sector Skills Council for Science, Engineering and Manufacturing Technologies' site looks at engineering, manufacturing technologies and science industries, covering fields such as aerospace, automotive, electrical, electronics, marine, mechanics, metals, science and bioscience. An overview is given of each and a careers progression planner, with factsheets about entry at five different levels.
Website: www.semta.org.uk

THE DIPLOMA IN ENVIRONMENTAL AND LAND-BASED STUDIES

The Diploma in Environmental and Land-based Studies was introduced in September 2009 and has been designed to give you a broad introduction to the industry. It will develop your understanding and awareness of the following areas:

- quality, supply and health and safety in the food sector
- sustainable uses of resources in the energy sector
- protecting our heritage
- quality of life in the land use sector.

The Diploma in Environmental and Land-based Studies may be for you if you want to gain knowledge and develop skills in these sectors. The principal learning that underpins the Diploma will provide you with appropriate skills as at least half the principal learning must be in the context of the environment and land-based industries. You will get the opportunity to experience and engage with real-world environmental and land-based activities and work with people from these sectors.

The Diploma in Environmental and Land-based Studies at Foundation level

The Foundation Diploma offers a new way into the environmental and land-based sector if you are at Level 1. The Foundation Diploma may be suitable if you are not yet ready for a Level 2 course but would benefit from an engaging programme that still provides clear routes to a wide range of Level 2 options.

The principal learning component of the Foundation Diploma in Environmental and Land-based Studies will provide you with a broad knowledge base relevant to the environment, and the applied learning will give you the hands-on experience that equips you with valuable transferable skills.

Principal learning themes

Three themes underpin the principal learning in the Foundation Diploma.

Productive and working environments
You will learn about:

- the different work environments in the natural world.

You could show what you have learned by:

- researching the impact of the weather on different working environments.

Plants and animals

You will learn about:

- different animal habitats.

You could show what you have learned by:

- making a study of the differences between a domesticated cat and a cat living in the wild.

Developing the sustainable environment

You will learn about:

- the different sources of energy we use.

You could show what you have learned by:

- looking at environmentally sustainable ways to conserve energy both at home and at school or college.

Principal learning topics

At Foundation level, there are six topics included in the principal learning as follows.

Components of the natural environment

This topic includes:

- the key features of habitats on land and in lakes, rivers and oceans
- the influence of weather on the environment.

Environmental and land-based production, systems and services

This topic includes:

- the meaning of the terms 'land use' and 'production' in the environmental and land-based sector
- how humans affect environments over time.

Introduction to working in the environmental and land-based sectors

This topic includes:

- jobs, training and qualifications for those who want to work or volunteer in the environmental and land-based sector
- the importance of health and safety.

Working with plants and animals

This topic includes:

- the importance of both wild and cultivated plants and both wild and domesticated animals
- caring for plants and animals.

Introducing the role and value of plants and animals to society
This topic includes:

- the value of wild and cultivated plants
- the value of wild and domesticated animals.

Impacts on the environment
This topic includes:

- why sustainability is important to the environment
- how humans affect the natural world and the implications for future-friendly living.

The Diploma in Environmental and Land-based Studies at Higher level

The Higher Diploma will give you the opportunity to explore the environment and land-based sector in more depth, and may be suitable if you are ready for a Level 2 course and are interested in these industries.

Principal learning themes

Three themes underpin the principal learning in the Higher Diploma.

Productive and working environments
You will learn about:

- the threats to natural environments.

You could show what you have learned by:

- researching why importing plants from abroad needs to be strictly regulated.

Plants and animals
You will learn about:

- the animal and plant kingdoms.

You could show what you have learned by:

- identifying where there are local animal and plant conservation programmes or initiatives.

Developing the sustainable environment
You will learn about:

- how human lifestyles affect the environment.

You could show what you have learned by:

- researching how to recycle in the home and analysing the benefits to be gained from recycling.

Principal learning topics

At Higher level there are eight topics underpinning the principal learning, outlined below.

Environmental influences on ecosystems and production zones

This topic includes:

- a look at the range of factors that influence the environment, plants, animals and related land-based enterprises
- how plants and animals depend on each other and how they adapt to their environments.

Working in environmental and land-based organisations

This topic includes:

- a look at the range of organisations that make up the environmental and land-based sector
- the jobs, career pathways and opportunities available.

Plant nutrition, growth and breeding

This topic includes:

- the needs of wild and cultivated plants throughout their life-cycle
- the growth, breeding and selection of plants.

Animal nutrition, growth and breeding

This topic includes:

- the needs of wild and domesticated animals throughout their lives
- the responsibilities of owners and/or managers of wild and domesticated animals.

Plants and animals and their role in society

This topic includes:

- the use of plants and animals for commercial production, recreation and tourism and wildlife conservation purposes
- the use of plants for production, work, recreation and well-being.

The importance of a sustainable environment to society

This topic includes:

- the meaning and value of sustainability
- the uses of the environment and the impacts of environmental activities.

Environmental monitoring

This topic includes:

- why and how the environment is monitored
- sources of pollution and waste.

Sources and uses of energy

This topic includes:

- current energy sources, uses and the impacts on the environment
- the need for alternative sources of energy.

The Diploma in Environmental and Land-based Studies at Advanced level

The Advanced Diploma in Environmental and Land-based Studies may be suitable if you are ready to take a Level 3 qualification. It covers the care of plants, animals and the natural environment and combines applied and theoretical learning in a way that will appeal to you if you want to add breadth to your knowledge and increase your understanding of the environment and land-based sector while remaining in full-time education.

Principal learning themes

Three themes underpin the principal learning in the Advanced Diploma.

Productive and working environments

You will learn about:

- the kinds of businesses that operate in this sector.

You could show what you have learned by:

- designing a product that will facilitate recycling or sustainability and write a business plan for it.

Plants and animals

You will learn about:

- managing animals and plants in the wild.

You could show what you have learned by:

- choosing an endangered animal or plant from the wild and researching what strategies could be implemented to ensure that it thrives.

Developing the sustainable environment

You will learn about:

- ways that businesses can improve their sustainability.

You could show what you have learned by:

- surveying your school or college and identifying ways to improve its sustainability.

Principal learning topics

The following nine topics are covered in the Advanced Diploma in Environmental and Land-based Studies.

The ecology of the natural environment

This topic includes:

- basic ecological principles
- the importance of biodiversity.

The management of natural resources and resources for production

This topic includes:

- why natural and human-influenced environments need managing
- the practical skills required to manage animal and plant communities.

Business and enterprise in the environmental and land-based sector

This topic includes:

- the range of environmental and land-based industries and the career opportunities they offer
- business principles, structures and practices in the environmental and land-based sector.

Applied plant and animal science

This topic includes:

- learning about the basic structure and functions of plants and animals
- a look at plant and animal physiology – nutrition, reproduction and pathology.

Plants, animals and humans

This topic includes:

- the role and uses of wild and domesticated animals in the human economy
- environmental impact and environmentally sensitive areas.

Plants and animals: safe working practices and relevant legislation

This topic includes:

- health and safety risks and how to manage them
- systems to support safe working practices across the environmental and land-based sector.

Sustainable development of resources

This topic includes:

- the balance between the environmental and economic viability of sustainable development
- the importance of environmental policy, planning, management and protection and the roles of the organisations involved in sustainable development.

Global impacts and the environmental and land-based sector

This topic includes:

- current issues in the management of environmental resources for a sustainable future

- the impact of changing natural processes in the environmental and land-based sector.

Research methods, skills and environmental analysis
This topic includes:

- the value of environmental evaluation
- the techniques, skills and resources required to undertake valid research.

ASL for the Diploma in Environmental and Land-based Studies

At each level, you can develop your own interests in the environment and land-based industries by choosing specialist courses relating to your subject interests and career ambitions. You have plenty of subjects to choose from – you could, for example, learn more about health and safety in using agricultural machinery and chemicals, sustainable food production or horticulture and tourism. Alternatively, if you are thinking of going to university you could choose subjects that will help, such as A level maths or science.

You could also broaden your study and other opportunities by opting for a subject that reflects one of your interests or career ambitions e.g. a creative subject, a modern foreign language or a humanities subject.

Given the importance of ASL and the broad range of choices open to you, it would be really useful to get impartial information, advice and guidance from a teacher or tutor. Specialist advice and guidance may be needed to help you to choose the right qualifications, and your school or college will be able to provide access to a Connexions adviser or careers adviser.

The Diploma in Environmental and Land-based Studies and where it could take you

A Diploma in Environmental and Land-based Studies will give you the knowledge and skills that you need for either further study, work or training in the sector.

The environmental and land-based studies sector spans a huge range of professions and the scope of jobs available is vast and includes:

- guide dog trainer
- zoo keeper
- environmental scientist
- garden centre manager
- florist
- estate worker

- game keeper
- animal rescue worker
- forester.

It could lead you to a university degree in subjects such as environmental science or horticulture. There are also good opportunities for self-employment and you could start up your own business, for example as a landscape gardener or florist.

Additionally, because the Diploma in Environmental and Land-based Studies teaches a combination of subjects and helps you develop transferable skills recognised by colleges, universities and employers, you will also be able to consider opportunities outside the sector.

What environmental and land-based studies students have to say about their courses

'It's amazing how much I'm learning, far more than if I was in a classroom all of the time!'

'I'm learning how to get on with lots of different types of people. I think I have got more confidence too, because I've had to talk to lots of different people in jobs.'

Further information

To find out more about the Diploma in Environmental and Land-based Studies, speak to your teacher or careers adviser.

You can also find more information about Diplomas on these websites:

- www.direct.gov.uk/diplomas
- www.connexions-direct.com
- www.diplomaelbs.co.uk

If you'd like to find out where you can study for this Diploma in your area, you can visit http://yp.direct.gov.uk/14-19prospectus

If you would like more information about the environmental and land-based sector you could refer to the following resources.

Title: Growcareers
Overview: Growcareers provides information on horticultural specialisms and career profiles, with an excellent careers information pack available.
Website: www.growcareers.info

Title: Environmental Careers
Overview: This website allows you to research options before university, and read sector profiles, job profiles and case studies.
Website: www.environmentalcareers.org.uk/careers

Title: Land Force
Overview: Land Force is a one-stop job site specialising in the land-based industries.
Website: www.land-force.com/pages/careers.aspx

THE DIPLOMA IN HAIR AND BEAUTY STUDIES

The Diploma in Hair and Beauty Studies was introduced in September 2009 and is designed to give you a broad introduction to the industry. It will also develop your understanding of a wide range of opportunities in the sector; for example, work on cruise ships, theatrical make-up or being beauty editor on a magazine.

The Diploma in Hair and Beauty Studies may be for you if you want to gain knowledge and develop skills in these sectors. The principal learning underpinning the Diploma in Hair and Beauty Studies will provide you with these skills, as at least 50% of the principal learning must involve relevant activities in a hair and beauty context. You will get the chance to gain work experience and meet professionals in the field.

Did you know?

The Diploma in Hair and Beauty Studies is not intended to make you work-ready, but will instead give you the opportunity to develop your potential and give you an insight into what is required if you work in this sector.

The Diploma in Hair and Beauty Studies at Foundation level

The Foundation Diploma in Hair and Beauty Studies will introduce you to the exciting, fast-developing world of hair and beauty. It may be suitable if you are not yet ready for the demands of a Level 2 course but would benefit from an engaging programme that provides clear routes to a wide range of options at that level.

The principal learning component of the Foundation Diploma in Hair and Beauty Studies will give you the knowledge and broad base of skills relevant to the sector, and through the applied learning you will gain hands-on experience to equip you with valuable transferable skills.

The Diploma in Hair and Beauty Studies will teach you about the business skills necessary in the industry, for example how to run a salon and understand why communication and customer care is important. The Diploma lets you apply practical skills and you'll also develop the confidence to research and apply your knowledge of haircare, skincare and make-up techniques.

Principal learning themes

You will learn about:

- training, qualifications and career opportunities
- how culture and personality can be expressed through a person's appearance

- how to manage your hair, skin, hands and nails
- what affects consumer spending
- different job roles in a salon.

You could show what you have learned by:

- carrying out a job study by interviewing a member of the team in a salon to understand the responsibilities of their role
- giving a family member or friend, advice about skincare after carrying out an assessment to determine their skin type
- researching and identifying hairstyles that may be influenced by cultural beliefs and understand what they signify.

Principal learning topics

Principal learning in the Foundation Diploma in Hair and Beauty Studies consists of the following seven topics.

Introducing the hair and beauty sector
This topic includes:

- the size and structure of the hair and beauty industries
- the range of services and treatments offered in hair and beauty and the health and safety requirements.

Creating a positive impression
This topic includes:

- how to achieve a positive first and lasting impression and why this is important
- an opportunity to examine your own views and beliefs about personal stereotypes and perspectives of image and beauty.

Introducing hairstyling
This topic includes:

- an opportunity to practise selected hairdressing skills
- exploring historical influences, creativity, cultural hair diversity and hairstyling as an expression of individuality.

Introducing basic skincare treatments
This topic includes:

- the opportunity to practise selected basic skincare services
- an opportunity to consider and challenge perceptions of facial beauty, including a review of your own perception of facial beauty.

Introducing basic hand and nailcare services
This topic includes:

- an opportunity to practise selected nail service skills

- the key technological developments in nail services and how these have influenced the modern-day nail industry.

Personal appearance, style and well-being
This topic includes:

- consideration of the importance of appearance and style and the impact of lifestyle on looks, health, well-being and the ability to perform effectively at work
- reflection on how lifestyle choices affect you, and opportunities for improvement.

Careers in the hair and beauty sector and related industries
This topic includes:

- learning about the range of career opportunities available in the sector
- the opportunity to compare yourself against employer expectations in this and/ or other sectors.

The Diploma in Hair and Beauty Studies at Higher level

The Higher Diploma will give you the opportunity to explore the hair and beauty sector and develop and apply a range of practical skills, such as facial treatments, hand and nailcare and hairstyling, as well as a knowledge of the six industries in this sector.

At Higher level, the principal learning will increase your understanding of the hair and beauty sector. You will have a wide range of opportunities, not only in the sector but also through routes into **further education** and other lines of learning.

The Higher Diploma in Hair and Beauty Studies may be suitable if you are ready for Level 2 and interested in these industries.

Principal learning themes
You will learn about:

- the different professions in detail
- cultural and diversity issues, the science, anatomy and physiology involved, and the different consultation techniques used for each industry.

You could show what you have learned by:

- studying how make-up and hairstyling has changed through history and identifying key influences
- researching the type of assessments carried out in the different hair and beauty sectors and devising your own assessment to meet the needs of a particular client group e.g. men
- choosing a character from history, fashion or the pop world and studying their changing style and influences.

Principal learning topics

The following 10 topics are covered in the principal learning for the Higher Diploma in Hair and Beauty Studies.

Safe and healthy working practices

This topic includes:

- awareness of industry's personal hygiene, dress code and well-being expectations
- learning about the key safe and hygienic working practices necessary to deliver hair and beauty services.

The world of hair and beauty

This topic includes:

- learning about hair and beauty product design, development and supply
- a look at how the hair and beauty industries promote themselves and their products, and how this influences purchasing decisions.

The science of hair and beauty

This topic includes:

- the common testing processes used in the hair and beauty sector
- the factors that can affect the condition of the skin, hair and nails.

Communication and client care

This topic includes:

- learning about the range of transferable communication skills needed in the hair and beauty industries
- the importance of communication skills in building a successful career.

History of hair and beauty in society

This topic includes:

- historical influences on the hair and beauty sector, its services and trends
- landmarks in the development of the hair and beauty sector.

Promoting and selling products and services by professional recommendation

This topic includes:

- basic aspects of promoting and selling by professional recommendation and why these activities are essential to business success
- the impact of legislation on selling and promotion activities, in the hair and beauty industries in particular.

Salon business systems and processes

This topic includes:

- the operation of basic business systems and processes used in a salon reception function
- the basic range of transferable, commercial business skills and knowledge.

Exploring skincare and make-up

This topic includes:

- a look at how personality, culture, race, gender, fashion and religious influences can be expressed through various skincare and make-up techniques
- an opportunity to practise a range of basic skincare and make-up routines.

Exploring haircare and styling

This topic includes:

- an opportunity to look at and demonstrate how personality, culture, race, gender, fashion and religious influences can be expressed through various hairstyling techniques
- an opportunity to practise a range of basic haircare and styling services.

Exploring handcare and nail art

This topic includes:

- exploration of the nail industry's rapid growth
- an opportunity to look at how personality, culture, race, gender, fashion and religious influences can be expressed through hand and nail art techniques.

The Diploma in Hair and Beauty Studies at Advanced level

The Advanced Diploma helps you develop an in-depth understanding of the industry and lets you research the range of employment opportunities. It will also give you hands-on experience of the creative and dynamic hair and beauty sector. If you have the ability to achieve a Level 3 qualification, the Diploma will allow you to develop and apply your knowledge, skills and understanding in a range of contexts and offer you a variety of progression routes, including university, employment, training and Level 4 qualifications.

The principal learning for the Advanced Diploma in Hair and Beauty Studies aims to fill the gaps in other hair and beauty qualifications by providing essential knowledge, understanding and applied skills relevant to the sector.

Principal learning themes

You will learn about:

- researching and evaluating the business, management, manufacturing and media areas of the sector.

You could show what you have learned by:

- organising and putting on a hair show that demonstrates the latest techniques and fashions

- researching how a new hair product is marketed and identifying the target customer base
- devising a questionnaire for parents or carers that can be used to research their perceptions of hair and beauty over the years.

Principal learning topics

Principal learning for the Advanced Diploma in Hair and Beauty Studies consists of eight topics.

Business location and design for hair and beauty

This topic includes:

- the factors that influence buying a business, business location and the interior design of premises to create the desired business image and a well-designed, safe environment
- research and evaluation skills in the context of business location and design.

Event management and enterprise for hair and beauty

This topic includes:

- developing research, planning and organisational skills and knowledge by planning, marketing, organisation, implementation and evaluation of a hair and/or beauty event linked to business start-up or expansion
- an opportunity to lead and work in a team and co-ordinate the work of others.

Product research, design and development in hair and beauty

This topic includes:

- an opportunity to explore hair and beauty product research, design and development processes
- learning how iconic and technological developments have contributed to sector development and their impact on consumer spending.

Exploring business management for hair and beauty

This topic includes:

- the key aspects of hair and beauty business management
- how the management and the behaviour of the management team affect a business and those in it.

Exploring media and image in hair and beauty

This topic includes:

- engagement with and evaluation of a broad range of media approaches
- an opportunity for you to create and present a physical image linked to a hair, beauty or nail-related technical skill.

Exploring the world of spas

This topic includes:

- examining the development, diversity, benefits and impact of services in the spa industry
- an opportunity to explore debates around the effectiveness of various treatments and the relationship between different forms of treatment.

Business planning and finance in hair and beauty

This topic includes:

- an introduction to the business planning process
- the risks and opportunities of running a business in the hair and beauty sector and day-to-day business accounting and finance.

Cosmetic science

This topic includes:

- cosmetic science, including chemistry and its application in the hair and beauty sector
- applying knowledge by making simple hair, beauty and nail products.

ASL for the Diploma in Hair and Beauty Studies

At each level, you can develop your particular interest in the hair and beauty sector by taking more specialist courses relating to your chosen subject and career ambitions. For example, you could train as a barber, learn theatrical make-up or study alternative health therapies. Or you might choose a subject such as A level English or maths that would help you get on to a university course.

You could also broaden your study and opportunities by opting for a subject that reflects another of your interests and career ambitions e.g. a creative subject, a modern foreign language or a humanities subject.

Given the importance of ASL and the broad range of choices open to you, it would be really useful to get impartial information, advice and guidance from a teacher or tutor. Specialist advice and guidance may be needed to help you to choose the right qualifications; your school or college will be able to provide access to a Connexions adviser or careers adviser.

The Diploma in Hair and Beauty Studies and where it could take you

The Diploma in Hair and Beauty Studies will give you the skills you need for either further study, work or training. It will help you to develop entrepreneurial skills by going on to an Apprenticeship or another work-based training scheme and is a first step towards a career in the sector.

The hair and beauty sector spans a huge range of professions and there's considerable scope in the jobs available. They include:

- hairdresser or barber
- nail technician
- beauty or spa therapist
- business manager
- make-up artist
- tattooist
- trichologist
- body piercer
- cosmetologist.

The Diploma could give you the background for a foundation or honours degree in biology, dermatology or even business management. Or it could help you begin a career as a hairdresser or barber, nail technician, make-up artist, spa therapist or business manager.

The Diploma teaches a combination of subjects, so you develop the transferable skills that are needed in education and employment regardless of what you choose to do, allowing you to keep your options open.

What hair and beauty studies students have to say about their courses

'I really like getting set challenges and having the chance to come up with solutions for myself.'

'Now I know I don't want to be a nail technician any more – there are just so many other jobs I am interested in. I am thinking of going on to university to study business management. I would never have thought of that before my Diploma.'

Further information

To find out more about the Diploma in Hair and Beauty Studies, speak to your teacher or careers adviser. You can also find out more about Diplomas on these websites:

- www.direct.gov.uk/diplomas
- www.connexions-direct.com

If you would like to find where you can study for this Diploma in your area, visit http://yp.direct.gov.uk/14-19prospectus

You can obtain more information about the hair and beauty sector from the following resources and sources of information.

Title: Habia
Overview: This sector skills website provides comprehensive information about the hair and beauty industry. Habia is the standard-setting body for the hair, beauty, nails and spa industries.
Website: www.habia.org

Title: Labour Market Exploration Hair and Beauty
Overview: This Labour Market Information briefing leaflet offers an introduction to the sector, detailing the numbers employed, trends in the industry and the skills required, as well as offering web links for further research. Go to the Free Downloads section of the website below and click on 'Health and Beauty' in the LMI Summaries section.
Website: www.iagworkforce.co.uk

THE DIPLOMA IN HOSPITALITY

The Diploma in Hospitality was introduced in September 2009. Through a combination of theoretical and applied learning, it will let you develop the knowledge, understanding and skills that are in demand in the UK and worldwide, working in a variety of different contexts. The Diploma in Hospitality allows you to progress to further or higher education, training or employment both in and outside the hospitality industries.

The hospitality sector includes a wide range of businesses, such as:

- hotels
- restaurants
- schools
- hospitals
- leisure events
- public houses
- contract food services.

Many of the sectors also offer exciting opportunities to work abroad.

The principal learning underpinning the Diploma in Hospitality will give you the industry-specific skills and knowledge you need, as at least 50% of the principal learning must be in a hospitality context and involve relevant activities. You will have the opportunity to gain relevant work experience and meet professionals working in the field.

The Diploma in Hospitality at Foundation level

The Foundation Diploma will offer you the chance to discover how hospitality affects our lives and you will develop the valuable transferable skills that are sought after in the sector, while keeping your options open.

The Foundation Diploma in Hospitality may be suitable if you are not yet ready for the demands of a Level 2 course but would benefit from an engaging programme that provides clear routes to a wide range of options at that level.

The principal learning will provide you with a broad understanding of the hospitality industry, the roles available in it and the skills and knowledge it requires.

Principal learning themes

The following three themes underpin principal learning in the Foundation Diploma in Hospitality.

The hospitality industry
You will learn about:

- the different aspects of the industry.

You could show what you have learned by:

- mapping the local hospitality provision in your area and identifying the range of provision and service.

People in hospitality
You will learn about:

- how hospitality is a customer-centred business.

You could show what you have learned by:

- role-playing a positive and negative customer service experience in a hospitality context.

Hospitality operations
You will learn about:

- the importance of food preparation and presentation.

You could show what you have learned by:

- preparing a celebratory meal, from designing a theme and planning a menu through to preparing, cooking and serving the meal.

Principal learning topics
The three themes of the Foundation Diploma in Hospitality are delivered through the four topics described below.

Introducing the UK hospitality industry
This topic includes:

- learning about the hospitality industry in the UK
- the broad range of hospitality establishments in the UK.

Introducing customer service
This topic includes:

- the personal responsibility needed to work in the industry
- the range of customer services delivered by hospitality establishments.

Developing skills to work in the hospitality industry
This topic includes:

- learning about the importance of team working and communication
- the range of communication methods used in hospitality and how customers' needs are communicated.

Preparing and serving food and beverages
This topic includes:

- the range of food types and drinks served in hospitality establishments in the UK
- the basic terminology used to define food, cooking methods and cooking equipment.

The Diploma in Hospitality at Higher level

The Higher Diploma will give you the opportunity to explore the growing hospitality sector and develop and apply a range of practical skills required in the hospitality industries.

At Higher level, principal learning will provide you with a more in-depth understanding of the sector. It offers a wide range of progression opportunities, not just in the sector but also into further education, other lines of learning and employment or training.

The Higher Diploma in Hospitality may be suitable if you are ready for Level 2 learning and interested in this sector.

Principal learning themes

The four themes that underpin principal learning in the Higher Diploma are as follows.

The hospitality industry

You will learn about:

- how the law affects the industry.

You could show what you have learned by:

- investigating the new building regulations for hotels and bed and breakfast establishments.

People in hospitality

You will learn about:

- the principles of healthy eating.

You could show what you have learned by:

- researching and creating a food product that is suitable for those with allergies or intolerances.

Hospitality operations

You will learn about:

- the importance of communication in the industry.

You could show what you have learned by:

- compiling a survey to use with hospitality providers to determine how they market their services locally and nationally.

Business and finance in hospitality

You will learn about:

- the basics of financial management.

You could show what you have learned by:

- organising a festival, putting together a budget and working out ticket costs and gross profit.

Principal learning topics

At Higher level, the following seven principal learning topics aim to provide the knowledge and skills that underpin employment in the sector.

Exploring the UK hospitality industry

This topic includes:

- the size and range of jobs in the UK hospitality industry
- the terminology used in the hospitality sectors.

Customer service in hospitality

This topic includes:

- learning how hospitality organisations provide good customer service
- how customer service is monitored and measured in the hospitality industry.

Working safely in hospitality

This topic includes:

- learning about legislation and regulations in the hospitality industry
- the implications of a number of important pieces of industry legislation.

Working in a hospitality team

This topic includes:

- the importance of team working in the hospitality industry
- the different roles in a hospitality team.

Dealing with costs and income in hospitality

This topic includes:

- the relationship in hospitality establishments between income, costs and volume and their effect on profit
- the importance and use of basic budgets.

Providing a hospitality service

This topic includes:

- the range of food and drinks available from UK hospitality establishments, including those from different cultures
- the different methods of food and beverage service and how they vary between hospitality establishments.

Food preparation and cooking

This topic includes:

- the basic terminology used to define food, ingredients, dishes and cooking methods
- the range, use and maintenance of cooking equipment in hospitality establishments.

The Diploma in Hospitality at Advanced level

The Advanced Diploma will give you the opportunity to add depth and breadth to your skills and knowledge of the sector and prepare you for higher education or the world of work, whatever suits you best.

The Advanced Diploma blends applied and theoretical learning and will appeal to you if you are interested in exploring the hospitality sector while remaining in full-time education. The Advanced Diploma in Hospitality may be suitable if you are ready to take a Level 3 qualification.

If you decide to take this Diploma, you will have a wide range of progression opportunities, not just into the sector but also further and higher education across a wide range of subjects.

Principal learning themes

The four themes that underpin principal learning in the Advanced Diploma are set out below.

The hospitality industry
You will learn about:

- how the industry thrives on fresh ideas.

You could show what you have learned by:

- developing an idea for a themed child-friendly café and writing a business plan, including what you would need to do to get it up and running.

People in hospitality
You will learn about:

- how attitude is important to customer service.

You could show what you have learned by:

- role-playing a hotel reception situation in which a client's booking has been taken incorrectly and there are no suitable rooms available, demonstrating how to provide excellent customer care when faced with a complaint.

Hospitality operations
You will learn about:

- team working and management in the industry.

You could show what you have learned by:

- planning and running an event in a team at your school or college, allocating responsibilities such as management, design, planning, catering, ticket sales and marketing, budgets etc.

Business and finance in hospitality

You will learn about:

- how to analyse the strengths of a business in the sector.

You could show what you have learned by:

- researching an event you plan to hold to establish that it is financially viable and designing a questionnaire to support your case.

Principal learning topics

At Advanced level, the 10 principal learning topics aim to provide the knowledge and skills that underpin employment in the sector.

Investigating the hospitality industry

This topic includes:

- the size, range and importance of the hospitality industry
- the relationship between the tourism and hospitality industries.

Legislation and procedures in the hospitality industry

This topic includes:

- learning about the legislation that affects the hospitality industry
- the implications of legislation in hospitality.

Customer service standards in the hospitality industry

This topic includes:

- the range of customer services in the hospitality industry
- how the effectiveness of customer service is measured.

Building and developing effective hospitality teams

This topic includes:

- the essential characteristics, roles and responsibilities of hospitality team members
- how hospitality teams work together to provide effective customer service.

Managing people in the hospitality industry

This topic includes:

- the range of managerial roles and responsibilities
- how hospitality organisations recruit.

Finance and budgetary control

This topic includes:

- the relevant terminology used in financial and management documents – for example, profit margins and portion control
- how costs are managed by hospitality establishments.

Running a hospitality business

This topic includes:

- how to set up a hospitality business
- types and sources of finance available to hospitality businesses.

Sales and marketing

This topic includes:

- relevant marketing terminology in the hospitality industry
- how hospitality establishments identify customers' needs.

Managing a food operation in hospitality

This topic includes:

- the terminology used to define food, ingredients, dishes and cooking methods
- a range of appropriate advanced professional cookery principles.

Hospitality services

This topic includes:

- analysing how hospitality departments collaborate to provide effective customer service
- exploring potential career opportunities in the hospitality industry.

ASL for the Diploma in Hospitality

Choosing the right ASL is important, and at each level of the Diploma you will be able to develop your hospitality interests by taking specialist courses relating to your chosen subject and career ambitions. You could learn about how to market and manage an event, set up your own business or train to be a sommelier. Additionally, you could choose a subject such as economics or a language as an A level that would help you get on to a university course. You can also add breadth to your course by taking additional subjects that reflect your other interests and career ambitions e.g. a science, music or a foreign language. The latter can be especially useful in a sector with great opportunities to work abroad.

Given the importance of ASL and the broad range of choices open to you, it would be really useful to get impartial information, advice and guidance from a teacher or tutor. Specialist advice and guidance may be needed to help you choose the right qualifications, and your school or college will be able to provide access to a Connexions adviser or careers adviser.

The Diploma in Hospitality and where it could take you

Through the Diploma in Hospitality, you will be able to see the huge range of employment opportunities available in the industry. Your attitude and customer service skills will be important, and the Diploma will support you in developing your confidence and understanding what is involved in setting up your own small business – there are many opportunities to develop entrepreneurial skills in the hospitality sector.

The sector spans a huge range of professions and the scope of jobs available includes:

- concierge
- hotel receptionist
- conference and banqueting manager
- bar manager
- sommelier
- housekeeper
- room attendant
- publican.

A Diploma in Hospitality will give you the skills you need for university and could lead to a degree in subjects such as hospitality, events management or business.

The Diploma also teaches you a combination of subjects and will give you the transferable skills needed at colleges and universities or by employers – this means you don't have to opt for a career in the sector and you can keep your options open.

What hospitality students have to say about their courses

'I am learning skills that I might not have got on other courses.'

'You meet lots of new people. Entrepreneurs told us about how they started off in business.'

'I think I would like to be a hotel manager in the future – I might do an Apprenticeship after my Diploma.'

Further information

To find out more about the Diploma in Hospitality, speak to your teacher or careers adviser.

You can also find out more about Diplomas on these websites:

- www.direct.gov.uk/diplomas
- www.connexions-direct.com
- www.hospitalitydiploma.co.uk

To find out where you can study for this Diploma in your area, you can visit http://yp.direct. gov.uk/14-19prospectus

If you want more information about the hospitality sector, you can refer to the following resources and sources of support.

Title: Improve Skills – careers section
Overview: The section tells you everything you need to know about a career in the food and drink industry, how to get qualified and how to go about finding a job.
Website: www.improve-skills.co.uk/careers

Title: People1st
Overview: A comprehensive website for all 14 industries that make up the hospitality, leisure, travel and tourism sector. There are numerous links to other useful sites, including some outside the UK, underlining the global perspective of the hospitality industry.
Website: www.people1st.co.uk

Title: Hotel Management Network
Overview: This site is promoted as a one-stop resource for the hotel industry, providing a range of resources and contact details.
Website: www.hotelmanagement-network.com

Title: Careersbox
Overview: Search for 'hospitality' on this online resource to find a clip of jobs in the travel and tourism industry e.g. a chef and trainee manager with the Spirit Group. It is also possible to select a specific area in the country.
Website: www.careersbox.co.uk

THE DIPLOMA IN INFORMATION TECHNOLOGY

The Diploma in Information Technology was introduced in September 2008 and is designed to meet the challenges of the 21st century by developing highly employable and skilled young people. The Diploma will engage you in real-world business uses of technology, and you will explore how it can provide solutions, transform businesses and contribute to successful project management.

The Diploma is based on the three integrated themes of business, people and technology and will help develop your ability to work effectively in a business environment, giving you the knowledge and skills you need to help you to fulfil your potential.

The Diploma in Information Technology enables you to learn through a combination of theoretical and applied learning, developing your knowledge, understanding and skills in a variety of different contexts that are in demand in the UK and worldwide. The Diploma allows you to progress into further and higher education, training or employment, both in and outside the information technology (IT) industries.

The Diploma in Information Technology at Foundation level

The Foundation Diploma in Information Technology will introduce you to the fast developing world of IT. The Foundation Diploma may be suitable if you are not yet ready for the demands of a Level 2 course but would benefit from an engaging programme that provides clear routes into a wide range of options at Level 2.

The principal learning of the Foundation Diploma in Information Technology will provide you with knowledge and a broad base of skills and, through applied learning in an industry context, you will gain hands-on experience that equips you with valuable transferable skills.

The generic learning and ASL elements of the Diploma will provide you with skills that you can use in a variety of settings. The Foundation Diploma therefore provides you with experience of the IT industry while keeping your options open.

Principal learning themes

The following three themes underpin the principal learning in the Foundation Diploma.

Business

You will learn about:

- how organisations use and benefit from technology.

You could show what you have learned by:

- researching how a human resources department in an organisation maintains a database of staff records and what this is used for.

People

You will learn about:

- team working.

You could show what you have learned by:

- working in a team to prepare a presentation about how IT can help small businesses be more effective.

Technology

You will learn about:

- databases and why they are important
- how to create your own multimedia product.

You could show what you have learned by:

- designing a spreadsheet to keep records for a small business
- designing an employee database for a small business.

Principal learning topics

Four topics are covered in the Foundation Diploma in Information Technology, as follows.

The digital world

This topic includes:

- learning about how technology contributes to a range of organisations
- finding out how technology is changing the way that organisations and individuals operate.

Working with people

This topic includes:

- a look at the use of different media and communication channels
- assessing how different behaviours, personal styles and actions have an impact on effective communication and achievement of objectives.

Working with technology

This topic includes:

- developing skills in the basics of systems, databases, network connections and security
- installing and using a technology system for a specific purpose.

Multimedia

This topic includes:

- a look at the use of different digital media for communications in a range of business contexts

- seeking feedback from the target audience and making suggestions to improve the product.

The Diploma in Information Technology at Higher level

The Higher Diploma will give you the opportunity to explore the IT sector, understand the new uses of technology in business and develop and apply a range of practical skills, as well as learning about the industries in this sector.

At Higher level, principal learning will provide you with a more in-depth understanding of the IT sector. You will gain a wide range of opportunities to progress, not only in the sector itself but also into further education and other lines of learning.

The Higher Diploma in Information Technology may be suitable if you are ready for Level 2 learning and interested in this sector.

Principal learning themes

Three themes underpin the principal learning in the Higher Diploma, as described below.

Business
You will learn about:

- the basics of how to manage projects.

You could show what you have learned by:

- taking on a real brief to create a database that supports the running of a department in your school or college.

People
You will learn about:

- how to write proposals that focus on particular challenges or opportunities in a business using creative, investigative, interpersonal and numerical reasoning skills.

You could show what you have learned by:

- working in a team to design a program to help a small business write a business plan, including spreadsheets for financial planning.

Technology
You will learn about:

- how to make prototypes and test your product to ensure that it meets its specific purpose and users' needs
- the technical knowledge and skills needed in design.

You could show what you have learned by:

- using online products to design a website and post a blog about your Diploma's progress.

Principal learning topics

Seven topics are covered in the principal learning for the Higher Diploma in Information Technology, and detailed below.

The potential of technology

This topic includes:

- how technology contributes to the success of a range of organisations, including its impact on efficiency and competitiveness
- how technology is changing the way that organisations, individuals and society operate.

Exploring organisations

This topic includes:

- different organisational structures, cultures and roles
- the use of technology to support business processes, describing what technology is used and what benefits it provides.

Effective communications

This topic includes:

- experimentation with different media for communication
- the features of effective communication between individuals and groups, with a particular focus on understanding how teams work.

Skills for innovation

This topic includes:

- opportunities for improvement in a range of example business scenarios
- identifying a number of options for every challenge and opportunity.

Technology systems

This topic includes:

- the role of key components in a networked PC system
- designing, developing and testing simple systems (including programs) to meet identified business needs.

Multimedia

This topic includes:

- the use of digital media to meet different business-related objectives
- learning the technical knowledge and skills to enhance web pages.

Managing projects

This topic includes:

- learning about project management, including task breakdown and estimating timescales.
- key factors in the success or failure of business projects.

The Diploma in Information Technology at Advanced level

The Advanced Diploma in Information Technology lets you deepen and broaden your skills and knowledge of the sector to prepare you for higher education or the world of work, whatever suits you best.

The Advanced Diploma blends applied and theoretical learning, and will appeal to you if you are interested in exploring the innovative IT sector while remaining in full-time education. The Advanced Diploma in Information Technology may be suitable if you are ready to take a Level 3 qualification.

Principal learning for the Advanced Diploma in Information Technology will provide you with valuable experience of this dynamic industry and let you explore what successful project management is, how technology can provide solutions in business and the role that IT plays in the global economy.

Principal learning themes

The three themes that underpin the principal learning in the Advanced Diploma are described below.

Business
You will learn about:

- the way technology has affected society, organisations and individuals, with a global focus
- how the Internet and mobile communications have transformed the business world.

You could show what you have learned by:

- researching the history of the Internet and investigating how businesses use the Internet to grow.

People
You will learn about:

- the knowledge and the skills required to work effectively in a business environment.

You could show what you have learned by:

- acting as the training manager for a virtual company and preparing an induction training program for new staff.

Technology
You will learn about:

- integrated technology solutions for a specific type of user
- how to design and develop your own multimedia product using video, audio, music and animation.

You could show what you have learned by:

- designing a product and using the most appropriate media to test it and then taking it to market, considering the needs and technological abilities of the client group.

Principal learning topics

The following seven topics underpin principal learning in the Advanced Diploma in Information Technology.

The potential of technology

This topic includes:

- the role of emerging technologies in achieving organisations' goals in a number of sectors (including commercial, public and voluntary)
- how organisations and individuals use technology to innovate and to improve competitiveness and/or service.

Understanding organisations

This topic includes:

- learning about how different types of organisation have different objectives, functions, roles and responsibilities
- the principles of key technology-enabled business processes.

Professional development

This topic includes:

- learning about effective communications in business and assessing the use and implications of different communications media
- exploring differing personal styles and behaviours and looking at their impact on others in team or one-on-one situations.

Creating technology solutions

This topic includes:

- the role and interaction of key technology components, such as programming language and database systems, in a range of typical current business environments
- the principles of integration and interaction between different business systems, including an appreciation of interfaces, data structures and protocols.

Multimedia and digital projects

This topic includes:

- the use of different types of digital media to represent different content needs
- the principles of planning, designing, developing, testing and implementing multimedia solutions, including assessing business requirements and audience needs.

Making projects successful

This topic includes:

- the principles of project management
- key factors in the success or failure of projects, including technology-enabled solutions in real-world environments.

Managing technology systems

This topic includes:

- the principles of effective change management for technology systems
- the technical understanding and logical processes needed in assessing the impact of problems in technology systems and addressing them.

ASL for the Diploma in Information Technology

Choosing the right ASL is very important, and at each level of the Diploma you will be able to develop your IT interests by taking specialist courses relating to your chosen subject and career ambitions. For example, you could learn about how to design a website and why search engine optimisation is important to a business's success, or how to use digital animation when designing software and computer games.

Additionally you could choose subjects such as maths or statistics as an A level to help you get on to a university course. You can also add breadth to your course by taking additional subjects that reflect your other interests and career ambitions e.g. a science, music or a foreign language. The latter can be really useful in a sector that offers good opportunities to work internationally.

Did you know?

If you want to study computer science at university then it would be a good idea to take additional maths. It's a good idea to contact the admissions tutor at the university you are considering to enquire about the acceptability of your Advanced Diploma course.

Given the importance of ASL and the broad range of choices open to you, it would be really useful to get impartial information, advice and guidance from a teacher or tutor. Specialist advice and guidance may be needed to help you choose the right qualifications, and your school or college will be able to provide access to a Connexions adviser or careers adviser.

The Diploma in Information Technology and where it could take you

A Diploma in Information Technology will give you the knowledge and skills you need for either further study or employment, and can be a first step towards a career in the IT sector.

The sector spans a huge range of professions, and the scope of jobs available is vast. It includes:

- ICT manager
- software professional
- user support technician
- maintenance engineer
- network engineer
- network administrator
- systems analyst
- hardware engineer
- systems designer.

It could lead you to a university degree in computing, computer networking, information systems, business and information technology computer games software, multimedia or graphic design. Or it could help you develop entrepreneurial skills that will help you identify opportunities for self-employment in the e-economy.

Because the Diploma in Information Technology combines a range of subjects, it enables you to develop the transferable skills recognised by colleges, universities and employers. This also lets you keep your options open and means you don't have to opt for a career in the IT sector.

IT in the UK

The UK IT industry is a fast-growing and dynamic sector. More than a million people already work in it, and with growth rates of up to eight times the national average, there are plenty of exciting and rewarding career opportunities. IT is vital in just about every industry you can think of, from retail to sport and from music to banking.

What information technology students have to say about their courses

'It is not easy. I am on the Advanced Diploma and it is hard, but the tutors are really supportive and they help you to come up with solutions for yourself.'

'I think it's a good course for people who don't know what they want to do; it's a good foundation for whatever you want to do afterwards.'

Further information

To find out more about the Diploma in Information Technology, speak to your teacher or careers adviser.

You can also find out more about Diplomas on these websites:

- www.direct.gov.uk/diplomas
- www.connexions-direct.com

To find out where you can study for this Diploma in your area, why not visit http://yp.direct. gov.uk/14-19prospectus

If you would like to know more about the IT sector, you could refer to the following resources and sources of support.

Title: e-skills UK – careers section
Overview: The Sector Skills Council for Business and IT occupations has this website offering information, advice and guidance about the sector. There is also a set of specific job profiles.
Website: www.e-skills.com/Careers/Job-roles/2035

Title: Big Ambition
Overview: For those interested in IT as a career, this website includes case studies of inspirational people working in the sector, examples of jobs, skills needed and a section on higher education.
Website: www.bigambition.co.uk/14-16

Title: The Chartered Institute for IT – careers section
Overview: The Institute's website includes information on a wide range of IT-related occupations, case studies and profiles. It also gives hints for building a career in IT, getting your first job, selling yourself and freelancing. There is also information about IT-related courses and topical articles. Go to the website below and choose 'Careers' from the Qualifications, Training, Careers drop-down menu.
Website: www.bcs.org

Title: Women in Technology
Overview: This resource offers information about occupations using IT but is mainly a place to look for IT jobs. It also includes news articles with interesting information about the IT sector and profiles of female role models in IT.
Website: www.womenintechnology.co.uk

THE DIPLOMA IN MANUFACTURING AND PRODUCT DESIGN

The Diploma in Manufacturing and Product Design was introduced in September 2009. It aims to meet 21st century challenges in one of the largest sectors in the UK by developing highly employable and skilled young people. The Diploma will provide you with real-world experience in industries that include textiles, engineering, chemicals and food and drink, and you will explore how manufacturing is responsible for two-thirds of the UK's exports.

The Diploma in Manufacturing and Product Design enables you to combine theoretical and applied learning, developing knowledge, understanding and skills that are in demand in the UK and worldwide in a variety of different contexts. The Diploma allows you to progress into further and higher education, training or employment both in and outside of the manufacturing and product design industries.

The Diploma in Manufacturing and Product Design at Foundation level

The Foundation Diploma in Manufacturing and Product Design will introduce you to this fascinating world. The Foundation Diploma may be suitable if you are not yet ready for the demands of a Level 2 course but would benefit from an engaging programme with clear routes of progression to a wide range of Level 2 options.

The principal learning component of the Foundation Diploma will provide you with knowledge and skills relevant to the sector, and through the applied learning you will gain hands-on experience and valuable transferable skills.

The generic learning and ASL elements of the Foundation Diploma will set you up with transferable skills that you can use in a wide variety of settings. The Diploma at this level therefore gives you the opportunity to experience the manufacturing and product design industry while letting you keep your options open.

Principal learning themes

Three themes underpin principal learning in the Foundation Diploma.

Product design and science
You will learn about:

- the properties and characteristics of different materials.

You could show what you have learned by:

- researching and identifying sustainable sources of packaging and how this contributes to sustainable manufacturing and product design.

Business and enterprise
You will learn about:

- how manufacturing businesses operate and how they're affected by price, cost and competition.

You could show what you have learned by:

- preparing a report for a client and calculating the cost of manufacturing a product for them.

Production systems
You will learn about:

- the departments and job roles in one industry and the key laws that apply in the workplace.

You could show what you have learned by:

- researching how the use of different materials for a product will affect the cost of producing it.

Principal learning topics

At Foundation level, there are six principal learning topics, as below.

Introduction to manufacturing
This topic includes:

- basic economic principles and the range of career opportunities that are available in the manufacturing and process industries
- the environmental and social impact that manufacturing has around the world and in the UK.

Dealing with customers and suppliers
This topic includes:

- the importance of good customer care
- learning about the different needs and relationships of customers and suppliers.

Introduction to working practices
This topic includes:

- learning about key roles and workplace practices in the manufacturing environment
- the importance of developing skills to work as an individual and in teams.

Introduction to product design and development
This topic includes:

- the various stages of product design and development
- the impact of new technology on product design and cost.

Introduction to materials science

This topic includes:

- the various chemical, biological and physical properties of a range of raw materials
- learning about how materials are tested and analysed for a range of purposes.

Manufacturing a product

This topic includes:

- the opportunity to experience the manufacturing of a product or prototype
- the practical skills required to make a product.

The Diploma in Manufacturing and Product Design at Higher level

The Higher Diploma will give you the opportunity to explore the manufacturing and product design sector and develop your understanding of its legal, ethical and commercial aspects. You will be able to develop and apply a range of practical skills, as well as learning about the industries in the sector.

At Higher level, principal learning will provide you with a more in-depth understanding of the sector. The Higher Diploma may be suitable if you are ready for Level 2 learning and can also lead to a wide range of opportunities, in the sector and also in further education or other lines of learning.

Principal learning themes

The following three themes underpin principal learning in the Higher Diploma.

Product design and science

You will learn about:

- the various stages in product design and development.

You could show what you have learned by:

- putting together a product design specification for a new sports drink, taking into account environmental issues when designing the packaging.

Business and enterprise

You will learn about:

- how a manufacturing business is structured and how it uses financial records.

You could show what you have learned by:

- preparing a financial report that shows the income, expenditure, profit and loss for a small business.

Production systems

You will learn about:

- how to follow a design specification and contribute to safety and efficiency when manufacturing a product.

You could show what you have learned by:

- role-playing the manufacture of a product in a workshop or on a production line, demonstrating safe working practices and understanding health and safety regulations.

Principal learning topics

The principal learning for the Higher Diploma in Manufacturing and Product Design is delivered through the seven topics detailed below.

Running a manufacturing business

This topic includes:

- the opportunity to understand and apply the business administration functions required in successful manufacturing businesses
- the characteristics and critical success factors of successful manufacturing enterprises.

The global business world

This topic includes:

- the relationship between manufacturing businesses, their customers and suppliers
- the global environment in which manufacturing businesses operate.

Working in manufacturing

This topic includes:

- key organisational roles, responsibilities and the rights of employees working in manufacturing
- the professional support functions that affect manufacturing productivity and the organisation's eventual profit.

Designing and developing products

This topic includes:

- the opportunity to develop an understanding of the various stages of product design and development
- the characteristics and properties of materials that influence product design and how materials can be safely tested.

Materials science

This topic includes:

- the opportunity to investigate the physical, biological and chemical properties of materials and organisms
- basic scientific principles relevant to the structure of materials and their common properties.

Processing systems

This topic includes:

- the main production processes and systems applicable in manufacturing and the technology and methods used to maximise efficiency in these processes
- safe working practices in laboratories, workshops and on production lines.

Product manufacture

This topic includes:

- the opportunity to develop an understanding of product manufacture
- production planning, the use of lean manufacturing methods, the implications of wasting materials, resources and energy and the effect of these on the production process.

The Diploma in Manufacturing and Product Design at Advanced level

The Advanced Diploma will give you the chance to broaden and deepen your skills and knowledge of the sector and prepare you for higher education or the world of work, whatever suits you best.

This course is a blend of applied and theoretical learning and will appeal to you if you are interested in exploring the innovative manufacturing and product design sector while remaining in full-time education. The Advanced Diploma may be suitable if you are ready to take a Level 3 qualification.

In the Advanced Diploma in Manufacturing and Product Design, you will explore the manufacturing industry in more detail, and the principal learning will provide you with valuable experience of this fast-paced industry and support you in applying craft skills.

Principal learning themes

The three themes that underpin principal learning in the Advanced Diploma are as follows.

Product design and science

You will learn about:

- different development techniques used in manufacturing.

You could show what you have learned by:

- preparing a study of the different approaches to manufacturing and product design in the UK and Europe.

Business and enterprise

You will learn about:

- manufacturing and business principles and the implications that financial planning and cost management have for profitability.

You could show what you have learned by:

- carrying out a cost–benefit analysis of expanding the distribution of a product to markets outside the UK.

Production systems

You will learn about:

- how to contribute to safety and efficiency and minimise environmental impact when manufacturing a product.

You could show what you have learned by:

- considering the risk assessments that need to be carried out when manufacturing a product and developing a template form to use.

Principal learning topics

Principal learning for the Advanced Diploma in Manufacturing and Product Design is delivered in the nine topics outlined below.

Manufacturing business principles

This topic includes:

- in-depth understanding of manufacturing business principles
- the opportunity to examine the link between enterprise, leadership and successful businesses in relation to the environment and the long-term sustainability of manufacturing operations.

Customer needs and market requirements

This topic includes:

- the importance of accurately establishing customer requirements so manufacturers can design and produce suitable products
- the need for effective customer liaison and establishing productive relationships.

Supply chain management

This topic includes:

- the importance of supply chain management in satisfying customer requirements
- a variety of supply chain management problems and how to resolve them.

Management of resources and working practices

This topic includes:

- the key employment and operational practices that apply to manufacturing, including management of human and physical resources and health and safety
- issues of communications, functional relationships and the management of assets.

Research, development and the introduction of new products

This topic includes:

- design methodology and the practices involved in researching, developing and introducing new products in manufacturing today
- learning about how innovation is important to business and the principle of continuous improvement.

Materials science

This topic includes:

- the physical, biological and chemical properties of materials
- more advanced scientific principles relevant to the testing and analysis of materials, looking at their impact on processing, structure etc.

Production and processing systems

This topic includes:

- an opportunity to investigate further the main production processes and how technology can be used to maximise efficiency in manufacturing
- the process control methods and systems applicable to batch operation, both small and large-scale, and continuous processing.

Managing production and processing operations

This topic includes:

- the key organisational and management methods employed by industry to maximise productivity while minimising waste
- the environmental factors that influence the effective manufacture of products.

Quality assurance in manufacturing

This topic includes:

- why quality assurance is important to manufacturing businesses
- an in-depth knowledge of quality assurance system requirements and the skills needed in applying them.

ASL for the Diploma in Manufacturing and Product Design

Choosing the right ASL is important, and at each level of the Diploma you will be able to develop your interests in manufacturing and product design by taking specialist courses relating to your chosen subject and career ambitions. For example, you could learn about how sales and marketing are integral to the sector, CAD's effects on product design and technological developments in the textiles industry. You could also choose subjects such as maths or economics as an A level that would help you get on to a university course. You can broaden your course as well, by taking additional subjects that reflect your other interests and career ambitions, such as a humanities subject, a science or a foreign language.

Given the importance of ASL and the broad range of choices open to you, it would be very useful to get impartial information, advice and guidance from a teacher or tutor. Specialist advice and guidance may be needed to help you choose the right qualifications, and your school or college will be able to provide access to a Connexions adviser or careers adviser.

What manufacturing and product design students have to say about their courses

---

'If you put the effort in, you get the right results. I am planning to do the Advanced level Diploma next.'

'We are getting some good work experience. I have been to a local outside catering company and learnt about packaging for different food products. It is good to get out of the classroom to learn.'

The Diploma in Manufacturing and Product Design and where it could take you

A Diploma in Manufacturing and Product Design will give you the skills you need for either further study or work, and it is a first step towards a career in the sector.

The sector spans a wide range of professions and there are many jobs available, including:

- production manager
- ceramic worker
- cake decorator
- upholsterer
- quality control inspector
- baker
- wine producer
- dressmaker
- saddler
- quality control assistant.

It could lead you to a university degree in food manufacturing, printing, publishing, ceramics, textiles, process technology and management, or to further training. Because the Diploma in Manufacturing and Product Design teaches a combination of subjects required by education and employers, it also means you can keep your options open.

Further information

To find out more about the Diploma in Manufacturing and Product Design, speak to your teacher or careers adviser. You can also find more information about Diplomas on these websites:

- www.direct.gov.uk/diplomas
- www.connexions-direct.com
- www.manufacturingdiploma.co.uk

If you would like to find out where you can study for this Diploma in your area, visit http://yp.direct.gov.uk/14-19prospectus

If you would like more information about the manufacturing and product design sector, you could also refer to the following resources and sources of support.

Title: Semta
Overview: The website of the Sector Skills Council for Science, Engineering and Manufacturing Technologies covers industries including aerospace, automotive, electrical, electronics, marine, mechanics, metals, science and bioscience. There are sections about each of these including an overview and a careers progression planner with factsheets about entry at five different levels.
Website: www.semta.org.uk

Title: Make Your Mark Inspiring Stories
Overview: This site offers 29 case studies of young people who have set up manufacturing companies in a range of different sectors.
Website: www.makeyourmark.org.uk/inspiring_stories/?tag=manufacturing

Title: The Diploma in Manufacturing and Product Design – real lives section
Overview: Four case studies on this site cover people working in different manufacturing companies; Brompton Bicycles, C2M (UK) Ltd, Tate and Lyle and Princess Yachts. Each one highlights why the Diploma in Manufacturing and Product Design is a good route for progression into their company.
Website: www.manufacturingdiploma.co.uk/students/real-lives

THE DIPLOMA IN PUBLIC SERVICES

Public services are a big part of our everyday lives, being responsible for law and order, education, central and local government, the health service, social and emergency services, regeneration and development, leisure and the armed forces.

The Diploma in Public Services was introduced in September 2010, and if you would like to make a difference to people's lives by working in one of these fields, this course could be of interest to you. The Diploma will help you explore the world of public services and has been designed to support you in employment, training or education, including university.

The Diploma enables you to learn through a combination of theoretical and applied learning, developing your knowledge, understanding and skills in a variety of different contexts.

The principal learning that underpins this Diploma will provide you with industry-specific skills and knowledge, as at least 50% of the principal learning must be in a public services context. You will get the chance to experience and engage with real-world activities, to learn about issues that helped build the sector and to work with people from the public services.

The Diploma in Public Services at Foundation level

The Foundation Diploma in Public Services will introduce you to the wide range of opportunities in this sector. It may be suitable if you are not yet ready for the demands of a Level 2 course but would benefit from an engaging programme that provides clear routes into a wide range of options at that level.

At least half of your principal learning should be in an applied public services context, which will provide you with knowledge and skills relevant to the sector and also give you the opportunity to gain hands-on experience.

The generic learning and ASL elements of the Diploma will provide you with transferable skills that you can use in a wide variety of settings. The Foundation Diploma will therefore give you the opportunity to experience the public services sector while keeping your options open.

Principal learning theme

The theme underpinning principal learning in the Foundation Diploma is detailed below.

Developing, maintaining and protecting society
You will learn about:

- the various career opportunities in the sector
- local public service delivery.

You could show what you have learned by:

- completing a study of job roles in the different uniformed services
- through role-playing and team working, demonstrating effective customer service skills at a police station, in a hospital or fire station.

Principal learning topics

The principal learning for the Foundation Diploma in Public Services is delivered through the following five topics.

Finding out about public services

This topic includes:

- an overview of the broad range of public services, how they are paid for and the types of service they provide.

Finding out about local communities

This topic includes:

- learning about how public services are delivered locally, and how local communities' different needs can inform the types of public service offered
- how public services affect local community life.

Maintaining health and well-being in communities

This topic includes:

- learning about how public services help to maintain, benefit and improve health and well-being for individuals, communities and vulnerable groups in society.

Protecting our communities

This topic includes:

- the organisations that provide safety and protection, and learning about some of the situations in which protection is needed.

Developing skills to work in the public services

This topic includes:

- the behaviour, values and skills that are needed to deliver public services, particularly relating to communication, customer service and team working, and the challenges and rewards of working in a public service.

The Diploma in Public Services at Higher level

The Higher Diploma in Public Services will enable you to explore the sector and develop your understanding of its legal, ethical and community aspects. You will be able to develop and apply a range of practical skills and learn about opportunities in the public services, in both uniformed and non-uniformed careers.

At Higher level, principal learning will provide you with a more in-depth understanding of the public services through the theme of developing, maintaining and protecting society and the provision and delivery of public services.

The Higher Diploma in Public Services may be suitable if you are ready for Level 2 learning in this sector. The Diploma can lead to a wide range of opportunities, not only in the sector itself but also further education and other lines of learning.

Principal learning theme

Underpinning the principal learning in the Higher Diploma is an expanded version of the Foundation theme.

Developing, maintaining and protecting society

You will learn about:

- the role of public services and how different services are funded
- areas of conflict between communities for public services and proposed solutions.

You could show what you have learned by:

- devising a questionnaire for parents or carers to survey their perception of public services and how they have changed over the years
- researching how students' views from your school or college have affected the institution.

Principal learning topics

Principal learning for the Higher Diploma in Public Services is delivered through the following eight topics.

Exploring public services

This topic includes:

- learning about the development and delivery of public services
- understanding the contribution made to public services by public, private and third sectors.

Paying for public services

This topic includes:

- how money is raised to pay for public services
- how different services are funded.

Government and legislation

This topic includes:

- the way that the UK is governed at national and local levels
- the legislation that influences public services and the legal rights of individuals and communities.

Communities and public services

This topic includes:

- the different types of community
- the ways that communities are formed and how they can change over time.

Promoting and influencing public services

This topic includes:

- how individuals and communities can help shape the delivery of public services
- the importance of effective communication and perceptions of public service delivery.

Public services that contribute to health and well-being

This topic includes:

- learning about the concept of health and well-being at individual, community and national levels
- awareness of economic, social and personal factors that may affect health and well-being.

Public services that protect society

This topic includes:

- the underlying principles for protection services
- how public services must work together to ensure individual and community safety.

Working in the public services

This topic includes:

- the behaviour, values and skills needed to deliver public services
- communication, customer service and team working, including the challenges and rewards of working in a public service.

The Diploma in Public Services at Advanced level

The Advanced Diploma will provide you with the opportunity to broaden and deepen your skills and knowledge of the sector and prepare you for higher education or the world of work, whatever suits you best.

The Advanced Diploma blends applied and theoretical learning and will appeal to you if you are interested in exploring public services while remaining in full-time education. The Advanced Diploma may be suitable if you feel ready to take a Level 3 qualification.

In the Advanced Diploma, you will explore the range of job roles in more detail. The principal learning at Advanced level will increase your understanding of the sector through the theme of developing, maintaining and protecting society. You will also gain valuable experience and the chance to apply your knowledge, skills and understanding in a range of contexts.

The Advanced Diploma in Public Services offer a challenging blend of applied and theoretical learning that will engage you in evaluation of the principles and practices of public services. It offers a wide choice of progression routes in education, training or employment in or outside the sector.

Principal learning theme

The strands of the theme underpinning principal learning in the Advanced Diploma are set out below.

Developing, maintaining and protecting society
You will learn about:

- the principles and practices of public services
- how public finance operates and how political neutrality plays an important role in public services
- the principles of marketing in public services.

You could show what you have learned by:

- researching how government policies affect the financial management of public services
- working as a team to plan and implement a project that benefits the local community
- researching how public services are marketed and the reasons for using different marketing methods.

Principal learning topics

Principal learning for the Advanced Diploma in Public Services is delivered through the seven topics outlined below.

Public services and collaborative working
This topic includes:

- the range of public services and how values affect their planning and delivery
- learning about the public services in the UK and comparing them with models in other countries.

Community engagement and partnership working
This topic includes:

- seeing how public services work with diverse communities
- learning about how the specific and changing needs of communities are identified and met.

Accountability and funding for public services

This topic includes:

- the financial aspects of delivering public services
- learning about different methods of running public service organisations.

Leading effective public services

This topic includes:

- leadership theories and styles
- comparing and contrasting public service organisations.

People management and public service values

This topic includes:

- people management in public services
- learning about the varying approaches to building and developing teams in different public services.

Management of public service projects

This topic includes:

- project management processes, tools and techniques
- how project management can affect public service efficiency and effectiveness.

Marketing and public relations in public services

This topic includes:

- the principles of marketing and public relations in public services
- learning about effective communication between public service organisations and customers and stakeholders.

ASL for the Diploma in Public Services

Choosing the right ASL is important, and at each level of the Diploma you will be able to develop your interest in the public services by taking specialist courses relating to your chosen subject and career ambitions. You could, for example, take a first aid course, get involved with a local community project, become a volunteer or develop your ICT skills. It is also useful to improve your physical fitness in preparation for a public services course or career.

You could in addition choose a subject such as history, sociology or economics as an A level, which would help you get on to a university course. You can also add breadth to your course by taking further subjects that reflect your other interests and career ambitions e.g. a humanities subject, a science or an art and design subject.

Given the importance of ASL and the broad range of choices open to you, it will be very useful to get impartial information, advice and guidance from a teacher or tutor. Specialist advice and guidance may be needed to help you choose the right qualifications and your school or college will be able to provide access to a Connexions adviser or careers adviser.

What applicants for the Diploma in Public Services have to say about their choice

'I have always wanted to join the police service, and that's why I am going to do this course to give me some experience first.'

'I am not sure whether to go to university. I am thinking of doing the Advanced Diploma in Public Services with Business Studies A level so I can keep my options open.'

The Diploma in Public Services and where it could take you

A Diploma in Public Services will give you the skills you need for further education, university or work, and is a first step towards a career in the sector.

The sector spans a wide range of professions and the scope of jobs available is huge. It includes:

- firefighter
- police officer
- prison officer
- community safety officer
- coastguard
- the armed services
- store detective
- environmental health officer.

It could lead you to a degree in ecology, policing, business management or law. As the Diploma in Public Services combines a range of subjects, you will develop the transferable skills needed in education and employment and keep your options open.

Further information

To find out more about the Diploma in Public Services, speak to your teacher or careers adviser.

You can also find more information about Diplomas on these websites:

- www.direct.gov.uk/diplomas
- www.connexions-direct.com

If you would like to find out where you can study for this Diploma locally, go to http://yp.direct.gov.uk/14-19prospectus

If you would like more information about the public services sector, you could refer to the following resources and sources of support.

Title: Local Government Talent: Careers
Overview: This website offers a wealth of resources, including a skills match facility and more than 200 career descriptions.
Website: www.lgcareers.com

Title: British Army Jobs
Overview: This comprehensive site has sections on skills, a job explorer and a virtual training ground.
Website: www.armyjobs.mod.uk

Title: Royal Navy – careers section
Overview: A comprehensive website that covers jobs, lifestyle, training and health and fitness.
Website: www.royalnavy.mod.uk/careers

Title: RAF Careers
Overview: This interactive site includes games, challenges, videos etc.
Website: www.raf.mod.uk/careers

Title: Fire Service
Overview: Online resources offer information about jobs, personal qualities and attributes needed and the recruitment system.
Websites: http://extraordinary.direct.gov.uk
            www.fireservice.co.uk/recruitment

Title: Could You? Police
Overview: This comprehensive site details four routes into the profession, covering challenges and what it's like to work in the police and details of pay and entrance requirements.
Website: www.policecouldyou.co.uk

Title: Step into the NHS
Overview: Raising awareness of a wide range of careers in the NHS, this site provides a career mapper, videos and job descriptions.
Website: www.stepintothenhs.nhs.uk

Title: icould
Overview: This online resource provides films from people in all sorts of careers, and can be searched in a number of different ways.
Website: www.icould.com

Title: Skills for Justice
Overview: A wealth of resources are available on this site, including Labour Market Information, information leaflets, qualifications across the justice sector, careers choices, advice, video clips and audio information on various sectors.
Website: www.skillsforjustice.com

Title: The Unusual Suspects?
Overview: This publication offers a guide as to how different parts of the criminal justice system work.
Website: www.cjsonline.gov.uk/downloads/application/pdf/Careers_and_volunteering.pdf

Title: How to become ...
Overview: Short descriptions of possible jobs following a Diploma in Public Services such as court usher, prison officer, police front counter clerk, local government graduate and apprentice in local government among others. Provides details of competencies, wages, job description, training and qualifications.
Website: www.diplomainpublicservices.co.uk/Careers/Careers-Publications

Title: Civil Service – jobs section
Overview: This site lists FAQs about careers in the civil service.
Website: www.civilservice.gov.uk/jobs/background

THE DIPLOMA IN RETAIL BUSINESS

The retail sector is a big part of our everyday lives and is the largest private employer in the UK, with more than three million working in a variety of roles such as sales and marketing, buying, merchandising, distribution, business management and accounting.

The Diploma in Retail Business was introduced in September 2010 and is designed to introduce you to all aspects of retail. If you would like to work in an exciting, changing and growing sector, this qualification could be for you. The Diploma will support you in exploring the retail world and its range of employment opportunities, and learning about how to set up and run your own business. The course aims to let you develop the transferable skills and knowledge that will help you to progress into employment, training or education, including university.

The Diploma enables you to learn through a combination of theoretical and applied learning, developing your knowledge, understanding and skills in various different contexts.

The principal learning that underpins the Diploma in Retail Business will provide you with industry-specific skills and knowledge, because at least 50% of it will be in the context of retail business. You will get the chance to experience and engage with real-world activities, learn about problem-solving techniques in retail and work with people in the sector.

The Diploma in Retail Business at Foundation level

The Foundation Diploma in Retail Business will introduce you to this growing sector and develop your knowledge of the range of opportunities available. The Foundation Diploma may be suitable if you are not yet ready for the demands of a Level 2 course but would benefit from an engaging programme with clear routes to a wide range of options at that level.

At least 50% of your principal learning should be in an applied retail business context, giving you knowledge and skills relevant to the sector. The generic learning and ASL components of the Diploma will provide you with transferable skills that you can use in a variety of settings, giving you the opportunity to experience the retail business sector while keeping your options open.

Principal learning themes

The three themes underpinning principal learning in the Foundation Diploma in Retail Business are:

- employability
- retail-specific studies
- specialist options.

You will learn about:

- retailing and the retail environment
- how important it is to be enterprising
- the retail supply chain and how retail outlets work, as well as selling techniques and customer service.

You could show what you have learned by:

- role-playing to demonstrate good and bad customer service experiences and reinforce the significance of good service
- researching the range of different methods of selling and marketing, such as the Internet, shops, catalogues, radio and TV.

Principal learning topics

Principal learning for the Foundation Diploma in Retail Business is delivered through the six topics outlined below.

An introduction to retailing

This topic includes:

- the wide range of retailers in the UK
- the effect that retailers can have on individuals and communities, including employment opportunities.

Exploring enterprise in retail business

This topic includes:

- an awareness of the principles of enterprise
- the chance to develop your own enterprise capabilities through retail market research and the development of brand ideas.

Introducing the retail supply chain

This topic includes:

- the different stages in the retail supply chain
- the range of problems that prevent products from arriving with a retailer on time.

Introducing the retail outlet

This topic includes:

- the opportunity to experience the range of retail outlet activities.

Introduction to customer service in retail business

This topic includes:

- the importance of customer service in retail businesses
- finding out about the standards of service expected by engaging with different types of customer in a retail setting.

Introduction to retail selling

This topic includes:

- the opportunity to use experiences of selling in a real or simulated environment
- practising sales techniques and developing skills to influence buying decisions in different situations with different customers.

The Diploma in Retail Business at Higher level

The Higher Diploma will give you the opportunity to explore the retail business sector in more depth and develop your understanding of the practices and processes that are currently used. You will be able to develop and apply a range of practical skills as well as learn about opportunities in the sector.

The Higher Diploma in Retail Business may be suitable if you are ready for Level 2 learning and interested in the sector. It presents a range of opportunities, not just in the sector but also via routes into further education and employment.

Principal learning themes

Themes underpinning the principal learning for the Higher Diploma in Retail Business are:

- buying
- merchandising
- distribution and logistics
- customer experience and environment.

You will learn about:

- how external factors lead to change and research different approaches in retail
- how a retail outlet's layout and presentation affect sales
- how stock control systems and processes are used.

You could show what you have learned by:

- working as a team to develop a product and brand it, designing a logo and identifying the most appropriate way to take it to the marketplace
- researching a customer base and identifying whether the products they purchase could be modified or the range extended to meet their needs
- studying how and why different retailers merchandise their products in particular ways.

Principal learning topics

Principal learning in the Higher Diploma in Retail Business is delivered through the nine topics outlined below.

Exploring retail

This topic includes:

- learning about how retail businesses operate in a changing global environment where enterprise and innovation are key to success.

Exploring retail channels

This topic includes:

- how new retail methods are devised and operated, branded and promoted.

Sourcing and buying for product ranges

This topic includes:

- reasons behind buying decisions
- developing and applying the skills used to put together a product range.

Exploring the retail supply chain

This topic includes:

- what could go wrong in the supply chain and what supply chain businesses can do to minimise risk.

Operating the retail outlet

This topic includes:

- the functions and activities of a retail outlet
- developing team-working skills in a real or realistic environment.

Stock control in retail businesses

This topic includes:

- learning about why stock control is important to the profitability of retailers.

Customer service in retail businesses

This topic includes:

- learning what constitutes excellent customer service in retailing
- delivering customer service, and its importance for retail businesses.

Selling in retail businesses

This topic includes:

- the different sales situations in retail environments and how customer behaviour differs across these
- the impact of fraudulent sales and what can be done to minimise risk.

Retail theatre

This topic includes:

- learning about the range of different approaches taken by retailers in presenting their products and creating an enticing environment.

The Diploma in Retail Business at Advanced level

The Advanced Diploma will provide you with the opportunity to add depth and breadth to your skills and knowledge of the sector, preparing you for higher education or the world of work, whatever suits you best.

The Advanced Diploma blends applied and theoretical learning in a way that will appeal to you if you are interested in exploring the ever-changing retail business sector while remaining in full-time education. Through the Advanced Diploma in Retail Business, you will explore the range of jobs in more detail, obtaining valuable experience and the chance to apply your knowledge, skills and understanding in a range of contexts.

Principal learning themes

The principal learning at Advanced level will see you gain further understanding of the sector through the underpinning themes of:

- emerging trends driving the sector
- setting up and operating a retail channel of your own
- how visual merchandisers display products
- the theories and models of team dynamics.

You could show what you have learned by:

- taking and refining a product, reviewing its packaging and how it should be advertised, and writing a marketing strategy
- working as a team to role-play a sales team briefing, using different strategies that could be employed to increase sales and motivate staff
- researching a way to reverse the trend of falling sales for a product that has been in the marketplace for more than 10 years.

Principal learning topics

Principal learning for the Advanced Diploma in Retail Business is delivered through the eight topics set out below.

Examining the world of retail

This topic includes:

- learning why retail businesses must be aware of emerging trends affecting the sector.

Developing retail channels

This topic includes:

- learning about the many methods that retailers use to get their products to customers, from traditional stores to online selling and TV.

Buying practices of retail businesses

This topic includes:

- the role of the buyer in retail
- developing and maintaining relationships with suppliers.

Retail supply chain management and logistics

This topic includes:

- the retail supply chain and the journey of products from their source, through transportation and storage to disposal, including recycling
- learning about relationships in the retail supply chain.

Marketing in retail businesses

This topic includes:

- identifying innovative ways of developing marketing and advertising to increase a retailer's sales and market share
- learning about the enterprising and competitive nature of the industry, the marketing strategies of retail businesses and how to adapt these in response to external factors.

Merchandising in retail businesses

This topic includes:

- the role of the merchandiser and their importance to the success of a retail business
- exploring how a merchandising system can ensure that quantity meets demand.

Management of sales in retail

This topic includes:

- how retail businesses develop strategies to improve the customer experience and maximise sales
- time to practise and develop high levels of customer service and sales skills.

Visual merchandising

This topic includes:

- links with merchandisers to see how they use skills, resources and technology to develop visual merchandising from concept to installation
- opportunities to develop creativity and team-working skills that can be used in developing a visual merchandise installation.

ASL for the Diploma in Retail Business

Choosing the right ASL is important, and at each level of the Diploma you will be able to develop your interest in retail business by taking specialist courses relating to your chosen subject and career ambitions. For example, you could learn about fashion retailing, beauty products and ethical issues, distribution and logistics and sourcing trends and buying. You could also choose business studies, economics or a creative subject as an A level to help you get onto a university course. You can even add breadth to your course by taking additional subjects that reflect your other interests and career ambitions, such as a humanities subject, a science or a foreign language.

Given the importance of ASL and the broad range of choices open to you, it would be really useful to get impartial information, advice and guidance from a teacher or tutor. Specialist advice and guidance may be needed to help you choose the right qualifications – your school or college should be able to provide access to a Connexions adviser or careers adviser.

What applicants for the Diploma in Retail Business have to say about their choice

'My mum was a shop manager for years and I sometimes used to go into work with her – that's when I thought I would like to do the same. I am hoping that my Diploma will help me be a manager one day.'

'I am thinking of doing the Diploma in Retail Business because I like the idea of learning in real-life situations and getting some work experience.'

The Diploma in Retail Business and where it could take you

The retail sector and its supply chain are constantly changing. The growth of the Internet, new manufacturing techniques, expansion of retail chains and economic factors have all contributed to making it more competitive than ever before, so the sector will offer you a challenging and rewarding career.

A Diploma in Retail Business will give you the skills you need for either further study or employment and is a first step towards a career in the sector.

The retail business sector spans a wide range of professions and the scope of jobs available includes:

- vehicle sales executive
- retail buyer
- retail merchandiser
- wine merchant

- jeweller
- customer service assistant
- retail manager
- personal shopper
- builders merchant.

The Diploma could also lead you to a degree in business and management, logistics retail buying or human resources.

Additionally, because the Diploma in Retail Business teaches a combination of subjects, it will support you in developing the valuable transferable skills needed in education and employment and allow you to keep your options open.

Further information

To find out more about the Diploma in Retail Business, speak to your teacher or careers adviser.

You can also find more information about Diplomas on these websites:

- www.direct.gov.uk/diplomas
- www.connexions-direct.com

To find out where you can study for this Diploma in your area, you can also visit http://yp.direct.gov.uk/14-19prospectus

If you would like more information about the retail business sector, try the following resources and sources of support.

Title: Skillsmart Retail
Overview: The Sector Skills Council for Retail runs this website, with a section on careers that includes details of how to get into the sector, job profiles and qualifications in retail.
Website: www.skillvm.com/sr

Title: National Guidance Research Forum: Labour Market Information Future Trends
Overview: This website provides detailed information on different sectors, giving information on numbers employed in each, skills shortages, types of role, qualification levels, future trends, regional information and a breakdown of the sector in relation to gender, ethnicity and age profiles.
Website: www.guidance-research.org/future-trends/retail

Title: Diploma in Retail Business
Overview: This site covers the Diploma in Retail Business, including information on diplomas at all levels, details of how to get into the sector, profiles of sample jobs, retail qualifications and progression routes.
Website: www.diplomainretailbusiness.com

THE DIPLOMA IN SOCIETY, HEALTH AND DEVELOPMENT

The Diploma in Society, Health and Development was introduced in September 2008. It is designed to support you in exploring the wide range of careers available and understand four key sectors and how they influence our society.

The course lets you learn through a combination of theoretical and applied learning, developing your knowledge, understanding and skills in a variety of different contexts. The learning is challenging and stimulating and includes project-based work, work-related assignments, work experience and visits with the opportunity to engage with professionals in the field.

The fields of society, health and development are important to the well-being of our communities as they concern everyone. If you want to make a difference to people's lives, this course could be of interest to you. It has been designed to help you progress into employment, education (including university) and training, either in or outside of the sector.

The four key areas in this sector are:

- the children's workforce – teachers, youth workers, play workers, nursery nurses and more
- the health industry – medical staff, health workers, healthcare scientists, physiotherapists, occupational therapists and more
- the community justice sector – community support officers and community police officers, probation officers, youth offending teams and more
- the adult social care sector – social workers, care workers and more.

The NHS, which is just a part of one of the sectors, is one of the biggest employers in the world, with over 300 different occupations available.

The Diploma in Society, Health and Development at Foundation level

The Foundation Diploma in Society, Health and Development will introduce you to this diverse sector and develop your knowledge of the range of opportunities available. The Foundation Diploma may be suitable if you are not yet ready for the demands of a Level 2 course but would benefit from an engaging programme that provides clear routes to a wide range of options at that level.

At least 50% of your principal learning should be in an applied context and will provide you with sector-specific knowledge and skills. The generic learning and ASL parts of the Diploma will also provide you with transferable skills, so the Foundation Diploma gives you the opportunity to experience the four key areas while keeping your options open.

Principal learning themes

The principal learning in the Foundation Diploma in Society, Health and Development is underpinned by three themes, as outlined below.

Principles and values in practice
You will learn about:

- how an organisation can apply its values in everyday work and develop the skills essential to this.

You could show what you have learned by:

- researching the code of ethics or principles that underpin an organisation's work
- role-playing in teams to demonstrate your understanding of the communication needs of different groups of people.

Partnership working
You will learn about:

- how different organisations and services work together.

You could show what you have learned by:

- investigating the referral systems used by the emergency services.

Communication and information sharing
You will learn about:

- various ways of informing the general public about issues that concern them.

You could show what you have learned by:

- studying a public health risk (such as swine flu or avian flu) and identifying how health professionals and the government communicate the risks and prevention measures.

Principal learning topics

The principal learning for the Foundation Diploma in Society, Health and Development is delivered through the following eight topics.

A background to the sectors
This topic includes:

- learning about the structure, purpose and practical workings of the children and young people's workforce, adult social care, community justice and health fields.

Introduction to principles and values
This topic includes:

- learning about the principles and values that underpin the children and young people's workforce, adult social care, community justice and health settings.

Introduction to partnership working

This topic includes:

- learning about the types and purposes of partnership working in the children and young people's workforce, adult social care, community justice and health settings.

Communication

This topic includes:

- learning about why it is necessary to be able to use different methods of communication in the children and young people's workforce, adult social care, community justice and health settings.

Working safely to protect individuals

This topic includes:

- the opportunity to learn about different types of risk and understand the importance of maintaining a safe environment.

Health, well-being and lifestyle of individuals

This topic includes:

- the opportunity to explore the ways in which health, well-being and lifestyle can affect quality of life.

Addressing the needs of individuals

This topic includes:

- learning about the needs of individuals and how these are addressed by the children and young people's workforce, adult social care, community justice and health professions.

Human growth and development

This topic includes:

- the opportunity to learn about the stages of human growth and development.

The Diploma in Society, Health and Development at Higher level

The Higher Diploma will give you the opportunity to explore the society, health and development fields in more depth and develop your understanding of the practices and processes that are currently used. You will be able to develop and apply a range of practical skills as well as learn about the range of opportunities in the sector.

The Higher Diploma in Society, Health and Development may be suitable if you are ready for Level 2 learning and interested in this sector. It will offer you a wide range of opportunities in further education, employment and training both in and outside the sector.

Principal learning themes

The principal learning in the Higher Diploma in Society, Health and Development is underpinned by three themes, as set out below.

Principles and values in practice

You will learn about:

- the principles and values of different organisations and how these are applied in everyday work.

You could show what you have learned by:

- role-playing an induction training session for staff covering the principles and values of the organisation.

Partnership working

You will learn about:

- partnership working and team working.

You could show what you have learned by:

- completing a referral form for a young person who has been made homeless to help them access emergency advice and housing.

Communication and information sharing

You will learn about:

- different ways of communicating with the community about issues that concern them.

You could show what you have learned by:

- devising a parent/carer questionnaire to survey their perceptions of how crime in the local community has changed over the years and what could be causing this.

Principal learning topics

Principal learning for the Higher Diploma in Society, Health and Development is delivered through the following nine topics.

Principles, values and personal development

This topic includes:

- learning about the key values, principles, legislation and codes of practice that underpin good practice in the key areas of the sector.

Communication and partnership working

This topic includes:

- the opportunity to develop an understanding of how and why communication, information sharing and partnership working are important in the key areas of the sector.

Safeguarding and protecting individuals

This topic includes:

- developing an understanding of the importance of responsibility for personal health, safety, security and risk assessment in the key areas of the sector.

Growth, development and lifestyles

This topic includes:

- learning about how human growth and development and the health, well-being and lifestyle of individuals affect service provision in the key areas of the sector.

Addressing needs

This topic includes:

- learning about how services address the needs and preferences of individuals, families, carers, groups and communities through the use of assessment, planning, implementation and review.

Antisocial and offending behaviour

This topic includes:

- an introduction to the community justice sector
- a look at the causes and impacts of antisocial and offending behaviour.

Supporting children and young people

This topic includes:

- the work of the children and young people's workforce in supporting the development of children and young people
- a look at the range of services available.

Patient-centred health

This topic includes:

- the patient-centred nature of work in the health sector
- a look at how common health conditions are supported.

The social model of disability

This topic includes:

- an introduction to the social model of disability and its aims, objectives and meaning.

The Diploma in Society, Health and Development at Advanced level

The Advanced Diploma in Society, Health and Development will let you deepen and broaden your skills and knowledge of the sector, investigating the values underpinning professionals' work and the problem-based learning approaches used in the key areas of this sector.

At Advanced level, the Diploma will provide you with valuable experience and the chance to apply your knowledge, skills and understanding in a range of contexts. Its blend of applied and theoretical learning will appeal to you if you are interested in exploring the fields of society, health and development while remaining in full-time education and prepare you well for higher education, training or the world of work, whatever suits you best.

Principal learning themes

Principal learning in the Advanced Diploma in Society, Health and Development is underpinned by the three themes outlined below.

Partnership working

You will learn about:

- partnership working and team working.

You could show what you have learned by:

- studying an organisation whose commissioned delivery is changing for economic or political reasons, and then planning a workforce development strategy
- reviewing a local nursery or care home and reporting on how staff work together to meet the needs of the service users.

Communication and information sharing

You will learn about:

- communication and information sharing within and across organisations in the sector.

You could show what you have learned by:

- researching data sharing protocol between several local organisations in society, health and development.

Safeguarding and protecting individuals and society

You will learn about:

- how vulnerable adults and children can be kept safe.

You could show what you have learned by:

- carrying out a risk assessment for a day trip for younger pupils in your school or college
- writing a safeguarding plan for a children's home, taking into account relevant legislation, statutory guidance and policies.

Principal learning topics

Principal learning for the Advanced Diploma in Society, Health and Development is delivered through the following six topics.

The sectors in context

This topic includes:

- the opportunity to research similarities and differences in the purposes, structures and practical workings of the society, health and development fields.

Principles and values in practice

This topic includes:

- learning about how the principles and values embedded in key legislation, regulations and codes of practice are important to the society, health and development fields.

Partnership working

This topic includes:

- the opportunity to develop an understanding of partnership working and how it involves individuals, colleagues, teams and organisations in improving service provision.

Communication and information sharing

This topic includes:

- learning about how effective communication, information sharing and record keeping are vital.

Personal and professional development in the workplace

This topic includes:

- the opportunity to reflect on how to improve your own practice
- identification of good practice and planning for professional development.

Safeguarding and protecting individuals and society

This topic includes:

- the opportunity to understand the importance of promoting and protecting the health, safety and security of individuals and society
- the opportunity to understand assessment of risks in the workplace and in communities.

ASL for the Diploma in Society, Health and Development

Choosing the right ASL is important, and at each level of the Diploma you will be able to develop your interest in society, health and development by taking specialist courses relating to your chosen subject and career ambitions. You could for example learn about learning through play, ethical issues and care in the community. Additionally, you could choose a subject such as business studies, biology or chemistry as an A level to help you get on to a university course. You can also add breadth to your course by taking subjects that reflect your other interests and career ambitions e.g. a humanities subject, an art and design subject or a foreign language.

Given the importance of ASL and the broad range of choices open to you, it's very important to get impartial information, advice and guidance from a teacher or tutor. Specialist advice and guidance may be needed to help you choose the right qualifications and your school or college will be able to provide access to a Connexions adviser or careers adviser.

What society, health and development students have to say about their courses

'I thought it would all be about health – it isn't. I have enjoyed learning about the criminal justice service, and I think I would like to work in the courts.'

'I used to be quite shy, but everyone says I now have more confidence in myself. I think the Diploma has helped with that.'

'It has opened up my eyes to all the different types of jobs I could do, but I'm going to university first.'

The Diploma in Society, Health and Development and where it could take you

A Diploma in Society, Health and Development will give you the skills you need for either further study or employment and training, and is a first step towards a career in the sector.

The sector spans a large range of professions and the scope of jobs available is huge. It includes:

- social worker
- play worker
- teacher
- healthcare scientist
- counsellor
- probation officer
- educational psychologist.

The Diploma could lead you to a university degree in childhood studies, dietetics, nursing, community justice, applied criminology or forensic investigation.

Additionally, as the Diploma in Society, Health and Development combines subjects and supports you in developing valuable transferable skills recognised in both education and employment, it will allow you to keep your options open and progress in or outside the sector.

Further information

To find out more about the Diploma in Society, Health and Developme
teacher or careers adviser.

You can also find more information about Diplomas on these websites:

- www.direct.gov.uk/diplomas
- www.connexions-direct.com
- http://shd.skillsforhealth.org.uk

If you would like to find out where you can study for this Diploma in your area, go to http://
yp.direct.gov.uk/14-19prospectus

The following resources and sources of support also provide more details of the society,
health and development sector.

Title: Step in to the NHS
Overview: A comprehensive website, this highlights a range of opportunities in the NHS,
and includes information on diversity and community, job titles, the benefits of the NHS,
the joy of caring and video clips about working in the service.
Website: www.stepintothenhs.nhs.uk

Title: NHS Careers
Overview: This site offers comprehensive up-to-date information about all careers in the
NHS, including an A–Z of different roles, downloadable leaflets and a course finder.
Website: www.nhscareers.nhs.uk

Title: Skills for Justice
Overview: Here you will find useful links to different areas of justice and case studies of
people working in the field. It also includes information on justice trends and advice and
guidance organisations that you can contact to discuss career options.
Website: www.skillsforjustice.com/careers

Title: Skills for Justice: Labour Market Information Matrix
Overview: Provides data on all aspects of the justice workforce, including police and law
enforcement, forensic science, prosecution service, courts and tribunal services, custodial
care and community justice.
Website: www.skillsforjustice-lmimatrix.com

THE DIPLOMA IN SPORT AND ACTIVE LEISURE

The sport and active leisure sector is growing quickly as a result of an increasing recognition of the importance of good health and healthy eating. People working in the sector have an important role to play in helping people stay fit and healthy.

The Diploma in Sport and Active Leisure was introduced in September 2010 and has been designed to provide a new and exciting programme of learning to ensure that the workforce of the future is able to encourage the population to lead active and healthy lives. The Diploma will support you in exploring the wide range of careers available and the different places you could work.

The Diploma enables you to learn through a combination of theoretical and applied learning, developing your knowledge, understanding and skills in a variety of different contexts. The learning is challenging, stimulating and includes project-based work, work-related assignments, work experience and visits and the opportunity to engage with people working in the sector.

The course has been designed to help you get on in employment, education (including university) or training either in or outside of the sector.

The Diploma in Sport and Active Leisure at Foundation level

The Foundation Diploma in Sport and Active Leisure will introduce you to this growing and exciting area of work and develop your knowledge of the opportunities available. The Foundation Diploma may be suitable if you are not yet ready for a Level 2 course but would still benefit from an engaging programme that provides clear routes to a wide range of options at that level.

At least half of your principal learning should be in an applied sport and active leisure context to provide you with sector-specific knowledge and skills.

The generic learning and ASL components of the Diploma will provide you with transferable skills, letting you experience the sector while keeping your options open.

Principal learning themes

The principal learning in the Foundation Diploma in Sport and Active Leisure is underpinned by three themes, as follows.

Sport and active leisure and the individual
You will learn about:

- your body, and the benefits of an active and healthy lifestyle, including positive risk taking

- the science of sport and exercise
- the effects of overeating, smoking, drinking and substance misuse.

You could show what you have learned by:

- carrying out an assessment of your fitness and writing yourself a personal fitness plan.

Sport and active leisure and the economy

You will learn about:

- the industry's profile in terms of size, scope and location
- the role and scope of regional and national bodies.

You could show what you have learned by:

- surveying local provision for sport and fitness and assessing whether it meets the needs of the community.

Sport and active leisure and the community

You will learn about:

- why the industry is described as 'people-centred' and what constitutes first-class customer service.

You could show what you have learned by:

- role-playing customer service in the sport and active leisure industry, highlighting the negative and the positive.

Principal learning topics

There are six topics underpinning principal learning in the Foundation Diploma in Sport and Active Leisure.

The importance of an active and healthy lifestyle

This topic includes:

- what an active and healthy lifestyle is
- a look at how lifestyle choices are made.

The importance of participation in sport and active leisure

This topic includes:

- learning about the physical and mental benefits of participation in sport and active leisure
- a look at the personal attributes and skills required to motivate and lead participants.

How the body works: introducing science in sport and exercise

This topic includes:

- learning about the basic scientific principles behind the human body and mind and how they respond to regular physical activity.

Introducing the sport and active leisure sector
This topic includes:

- a look at the structure of this dynamic sector
- the economic importance of the sport and active leisure sector.

Working with customers in the sport and active leisure sector
This topic includes:

- learning about how good customer service is important in this 'people-centred' sector
- developing an understanding of your own personal management and presentation to others.

Working with specific populations in sport and active leisure
This topic includes:

- a look at the specific needs of particular groups and how to adjust various sport and leisure activities to meet these needs better.

The Diploma in Sport and Active Leisure at Higher level

The Higher Diploma will give you the opportunity to explore the sport and active leisure sector in more depth and develop your understanding of the skills it currently requires. You will be able to develop and apply a range of practical skills as well as learning about the range of opportunities in this sector.

The Higher Diploma in Sport and Active Leisure may be suitable if you are ready for Level 2 learning and interested in this sector, because it offers a wide range of opportunities in further education, employment and training, both in and outside the sector.

Principal learning themes

The principal learning for the Higher Diploma in Sport and Active Leisure is underpinned by the following three themes.

Sport and active leisure and the individual
You will learn about:

- the behaviours and choices that influence diet, level of exercise, sleep patterns and substance misuse
- the basic principles of anatomy and physiology and their applications in the sector.

You could show what you have learned by:

- working in a group to assess the physical activity each of you participates in every week and recording it on a chart.

Sport and active leisure and the economy

You will learn about:

- the range of jobs in the sector and how its structure differs from place to place
- government policy in the sector and the responses of different businesses.

You could show what you have learned by:

- studying the different job roles in a local leisure centre or gym.

Sport and active leisure and the community

You will learn about:

- how to develop interpersonal skills and encourage repeat business
- the vital role of leadership skills and the principles of conflict resolution.

You could show what you have learned by:

- preparing a presentation to be delivered at a local fitness centre's open evening to encourage people to join.

Principal learning topics

There are eight topics that underpin principal learning in the Higher Diploma in Sport and Active Leisure.

Active and healthy lifestyle choices

This topic includes:

- learning about lifestyle choices and how they are important to a person's physical and mental well-being
- the implications of taking risks and the impact of sustained participation in sport.

Encouraging participation in sport and active leisure

This topic includes:

- learning about the range of different methods that can be used to encourage ongoing participation among different individuals and groups
- gaining an understanding of promotional strategies and motivational techniques that can be used at both an organisational and individual level.

Science in sport and active leisure

This topic includes:

- the basic principles of anatomy and physiology
- learning about safe and successful participation in sport and active leisure activities.

Working in sport and active leisure locally

This topic includes:

- the growing economic importance of the sport and active leisure sector
- a look at the huge range of careers available in the sector.

Businesses in the sport and active leisure sector
This topic includes:

- the range of business models that operate in the public, private and third sectors
- the key business practices and problems that businesses face.

Media in sport and active leisure
This topic includes:

- a look at the close relationship between the media and the sport and active leisure sector
- the impact of media coverage on sport.

The customer experience
This topic includes:

- learning about how customer service is essential to the effectiveness of organisations.

Access for all in sport and active leisure
This topic includes:

- learning about how sport and active leisure organisations work with the general public to ensure the opportunity to access activities.

The Diploma in Sport and Active Leisure at Advanced level

The Advanced Diploma in Sport and Active Leisure will provide you with the opportunity to deepen and broaden your skills and knowledge of the sector.

The Advanced Diploma will help you increase your understanding of the sector, providing you with valuable experience and the chance to apply your knowledge, skills and understanding in a range of contexts. Its challenging blend of applied and theoretical learning will appeal to you if you are interested in exploring the diverse fields in sport and active leisure while remaining in full-time education, helping prepare you for higher education, training or the world of work, whatever suits you best.

Principal learning themes

Principal learning in the Advanced Diploma in Sport and Active Leisure is underpinned by the three themes described below.

Sport and active leisure and the individual
You will learn about:

- the positive steps people can take to improve their lifestyles and the implications these choices have on society.

You could show what you have learned by:

- researching the support available from GPs to help individuals improve their health and fitness e.g. weight loss clinics, smoking cessation clinics etc.

Sport and active leisure and the economy
You will learn about:

- the sector's impact on the economy and how it promotes and increases tourism and enhances national reputation.

You could show what you have learned by:

- studying paid-for and free health and fitness services in your community.

Sport and active leisure and the community
You will learn about:

- the implications of equality and diversity legislation and the principles of inclusion
- how to respond appropriately and fairly to all customers' needs, taking ethical considerations into account.

You could show what you have learned by:

- mapping local health and fitness provision for people with learning disabilities and ensuring that adaptations are in place, compiling an information leaflet and making this available to local providers of care for people with learning disabilities.

Principal learning topics
There are nine topics through which principal learning in the Advanced Diploma in Sport and Active Leisure is delivered.

The impact of an active and healthy lifestyle
This topic includes:

- ethical considerations that inform lifestyle choices and the impact of these on the individual and society.

Effective management and leadership in sport and active leisure
This topic includes:

- the key management and operational principles, processes and skills that the sector works on.

Applying science to sport and active leisure
This topic includes:

- learning about how anatomy, physiology and biomechanics underpin many aspects of the sport and active leisure sector.

Applying scientific principles to enhance performance

This topic includes:

- learning about how scientific principles can enhance performance in sport and active leisure
- a look at performance enhancement.

The sport and active leisure workforce and the economy

This topic includes:

- how the sport and active leisure industry contributes to the national and global economy
- the structure and characteristics of the workforce as well as an understanding of the skills required to work in the sector.

Globalisation and the sport and active leisure industry

This topic includes:

- a look at how commercial globalisation affects the sport and active leisure sector.

Politics and policies in sport and active leisure

This topic includes:

- how government policies influence sport and active leisure at national and local levels
- what the legacy of a major sport or active leisure event is.

Promoting opportunities for all in the sport and active leisure industry

This topic includes:

- the principle of inclusion and the need to promote equality of access for all to sport and active leisure
- learning about the factors promoting opportunities for everyone, including legislation, attitudes and customer relationships.

Developing community cohesion through sport and active leisure

This topic includes:

- how the sector can positively affect communities in a variety of ways, from providing role models through to legislation.

ASL for the Diploma in Sport and Active Leisure

Choosing the right ASL is very important, and at each level of the Diploma you will be able to develop your interest in sport and active leisure by taking specialist courses relating to your chosen subject and career ambitions. For example, you could take a course in first aid, lifeguard training or football coaching. You could also choose a subject such as business studies, biology or chemistry as an A level to help you get on to a university course. You can add more breadth to your course by taking additional subjects that reflect your other interests and career ambitions e.g. a humanities subject, an art and design subject or a foreign language.

Given the importance of ASL and the broad range of choices open to you, it's highly advisable to get impartial information, advice and guidance from a teacher or tutor. Specialist advice and guidance may be needed to help you to choose the right qualifications, and your school or college should be able to point you in the direction of a Connexions adviser or careers adviser.

What applicants for the Diploma in Sport and Active Leisure have to say about their choice

'My brother did A levels and I know all about them; when I saw the careers teacher in my school I asked about different courses available, and she knew I liked sport so told me about this new course. It sounds really good, but I need to find out a bit more so I'm going on a taster day at my local college before I decide.'

'I am thinking about sports journalism in the future, so I might do the Advanced Diploma with A level English.'

The Diploma in Sport and Active Leisure and where it could take you

The industry is one of the fastest growing in the economy. It's a popular choice because many of the jobs can lead on to careers in other sectors; teaching, journalism and business management are good examples of these. By 2014, it is expected that around 100,000 jobs will be needed, and the London Olympic and Paralympic Games in 2012 are likely to require up to 86,000 volunteers.

Progression from the Diploma is wide-ranging, as the sport and leisure sector spans a huge range of professions:

- fitness
- play work
- youth work
- stadium management and safety
- outdoor opportunities
- sport surfaces.

This means that the scope of job roles is vast, such as:

- groundskeeper at a county cricket ground
- sports stadium manager
- coach at a national sports academy
- personal trainer
- events steward

- after-school activities club co-ordinator
- outdoor adventure instructor
- caravan park manager.

The Diploma provides a wealth of personal skills and knowledge that will benefit you whether you choose to go on to further study or straight into employment. With more than 200 different roles in the sport and active leisure sector, there are lots of challenging and exciting opportunities.

The Diploma in Sport and Active Leisure teaches a combination of subjects, so it will also help you develop transferable skills valuable in education and employment and enable you to keep your options open.

Further information

To find out more about the Diploma in Sport and Active Leisure, speak to your teacher or careers adviser.

You can also find more information about Diplomas on these websites:

- www.direct.gov.uk/diplomas
- www.connexions-direct.com

If you want to find out where you can study for this Diploma locally, why not visit http://yp.direct.gov.uk/14-19prospectus

More information about the sport and active leisure sector is also available from the following resources.

Title: Skills Active Careers
Overview: This easy-to-use website provides sections on Apprenticeships, other training routes and 14–19 qualifications. It explains all routes and levels available in both sports and leisure and health and development, with case studies from across the leisure and learning sectors.
Website: www.skillsactive.com/careers

Title: 1st4sport Qualifications
Overview: This is the website of the awarding body for the sports and leisure sector, detailing all qualifications offered, including 14–19 awards and the Diplomas in Sport and Active Leisure. It also offers information about qualifications that can be included in the ASL for the Diploma.
Website: www.1st4sportqualifications.com

Title: Careers in Sport
Overview: A useful careers information site that offers easy-to-use information about a number of different sports and careers. It includes an interactive 'career selector' that leads to career profiles and case studies developed from interviews with people working in particular sports and leisure careers and a link to the Sports IQ online resource.
Website: www.careers-in-sport.co.uk

Title: League Football Education
Overview: This site supplies information on football Apprenticeships, including detailed explanation and case studies, an outline of progression routes post-Apprenticeship and downloadable brochures.
Website: www.lfe.org.uk

Title: National Skills Academy for Sport and Active Leisure
Overview: A general website that provides information on skills, training and careers in sports and active leisure, with a good overview of training options and opportunities and a careers advice section that links to the skillsactive website.
Website: www.sportactivensa.co.uk

Title: Institute for Outdoor Learning
Overview: Website for outdoor education that provides a careers information section listing the range of opportunities and training routes in the outdoor education sector.
Website: www.outdoor-learning.org

Title: Leisure Jobs
Overview: This website supplies details of careers in leisure from entry level to management and insights into current labour market trends.
Website: www.leisurejobs.com

Title: The Institute of Sport and Recreation Management
Overview: The Institute's site contains a basic careers advice section for school leavers and graduates.
Website: www.isrm.co.uk

Title: The British Association of Sport and Exercise Sciences
Overview: This website has a section covering careers information and further study, and you can also download a copy of the booklet *A Guide to Careers in Sport and Exercise Sciences*.
Website: www.bases.org.uk

THE DIPLOMA IN TRAVEL AND TOURISM

The Diploma in Travel and Tourism was introduced in September 2010 and has been designed to provide a new and exciting programme of learning in these areas. It will support you in exploring the wide range of opportunities and careers available in the sector.

The Diploma enables you to learn through a combination of theoretical and applied learning, developing your knowledge, understanding and skills in a variety of different contexts. The learning is challenging and stimulating and includes project-based work, work-related assignments, work experience and visits, plus the opportunity to engage with people working in the sector. It covers a range of different fields in this sector, including customer care, transport systems, finance and currency, sales and marketing and sustainability.

The course has been designed to help you progress in employment, education (including university) or training, either in or outside of the sector.

The Diploma in Travel and Tourism at Foundation level

The Foundation Diploma in Travel and Tourism will introduce you to this exciting, growing sector and make you aware of the range of opportunities available. The Foundation Diploma may be suitable if you are not yet ready for the demands of a Level 2 course but would benefit from an engaging programme with clear routes into a wide range of options at that level.

At least 50% of your principal learning should be in an applied travel and tourism context, so you understand the breadth of this sector and get the chance to practise the skills that are needed in travel and tourism.

The generic learning and the ASL elements of the Diploma will provide you with transferable skills that you can use in a variety of settings, allowing you to experience the industry while still keeping your options open.

Principal learning themes

The Foundation Diploma in Travel and Tourism is underpinned by three themes.

- destinations
- customer experience
- changes and trends.

You will learn about:

- why and how journeys are planned and how to use information to find out about destinations
- how to look after customers and understand what good customer service is
- why good customer service is important to the travel and tourism sector

- the wide range of opportunities available in the travel and tourism sector
- how government policies and the economy can impact on the sector.

You could show what you have learned by:

- planning a trip to a local tourist attraction and researching the cost of different modes of transport
- role-playing as a group a challenging customer service experience and demonstrating effective customer service skills e.g. dealing with a client at an airport whose flight has been delayed
- devising a questionnaire for parents or carers to survey their travel and tourism experiences over the years and recording trends.

Principal learning topics

Principal learning for the Foundation Diploma in Travel and Tourism is delivered through the following five topics.

Planning journeys
This topic includes:

- learning about why people travel, the types of transport available and their advantages and disadvantages
- using information sources to plan journeys that meet customers' travel needs.

Destinations
This topic includes:

- learning about the use of information sources to locate and find out about local, national and worldwide destinations and visitor attractions
- investigating a local area to identify what it offers visitors.

Looking after customers
This topic includes:

- the importance of excellent customer service for organisations, their employees and their customers
- developing skills in delivering service to a range of customers.

Working in travel and tourism
This topic includes:

- the scope and structure of the travel and tourism sector
- the nature of the work involved and the skills and attributes required.

Creating and delivering travel and tourism products and services
This topic includes:

- the opportunity to demonstrate the skills that travel and tourism employers want, in particular communication and team working.

The Diploma in Travel and Tourism at Higher level

The Higher Diploma will give you the opportunity to explore the travel and tourism sector in more depth and increase your understanding of the skills currently used in the industry. You will be able to develop and apply your own practical skills as well as learning about the opportunities in the sector.

The Higher Diploma in Travel and Tourism may be suitable if you are ready for Level 2 learning and interested in this sector. It offers a range of opportunities for further education, employment or training, both in and outside the sector.

Principal learning themes

The Higher Diploma in Travel and Tourism is underpinned by three themes.

* destinations
* customer experience
* changes and trends.

You will learn about:

* the key features of different destinations and how they meet specific customer needs
* how the environment impacts on the travel and tourism sector
* the importance of travel and tourism to the economy
* the importance of excellent customer service and how legislation impacts on industry standards
* how the travel and tourism industry recruits, selects and develops staff
* the structure of travel and tourism organisations and how they respond to change
* the range of products and services in the sector.

You could show what you have learned by:

* researching a local town, finding out which town in Europe it is twinned with and comparing tourism in both locations
* surveying local travel and tourism providers to see how they evaluate their services, customer satisfaction and effectiveness
* studying the way tourism has changed in your own town through history.

Principal learning topics

Principal learning for the Higher Diploma in Travel and Tourism is delivered through seven topics, as below.

Destinations

This topic includes:

* developing your knowledge of the key features of UK and worldwide destinations
* the impacts of travel and tourism, and sustainable development practices.

The UK travel and tourism sector

This topic includes:

- learning about the broad scope of the travel and tourism sector
- the key factors that have affected the travel and tourism sector of today.

The customer experience

This topic includes:

- exploring the importance of excellent customer service for travel and tourism customers, organisations and employees
- learning about how legislation and technological developments affect service delivery.

Working in travel and tourism

This topic includes:

- a look at job roles in travel and tourism and how your career could progress
- understanding employment requirements, rights and responsibilities and how organisations recruit and select staff and manage performance.

The business environment

This topic includes:

- the structures and business functions of travel and tourism organisations of different sizes
- business opportunities, trends or pressures facing a travel or tourism organisation.

Promotion and sales

This topic includes:

- how and why organisations promote and sell products and services
- creating promotional materials and selecting appropriate sales methods.

Creating and delivering travel and tourism products and services

This topic includes:

- dealing with customers, suppliers and colleagues so you can demonstrate transferable skills
- planning and implementing an idea for a product or service related to any one travel or tourism field.

The Diploma in Travel and Tourism at Advanced level

The Advanced Diploma in Travel and Tourism will let you add depth and breadth to your skills and knowledge of the sector. It may be suitable if you are ready to take a Level 3 qualification and are interested in exploring travel and tourism while remaining in full-time education.

The principal learning at Advanced level will provide you with a more in-depth understanding of the sector by examining its principles and practices. The Diploma will also offer you valuable experience and the chance to apply your knowledge, skills and understanding in a range of contexts.

The Advanced Diploma is a challenging blend of applied and theoretical learning and will appeal to you if you are interested in exploring the diversity of the travel and tourism sector; it will prepare you well for higher education, training or the world of work, whatever suits you best.

Principal learning themes

The Advanced Diploma in Travel and Tourism is underpinned by three main themes.

- destinations
- customer experience
- changes and trends.

You will learn about:

- how UK and worldwide destinations can benefit from travel and tourism
- how tourists, travellers, communities and organisations can have conflicting needs
- how global politics, economies and the environment can impact on travel and tourism
- the role of technology and the importance of new technologies in the travel and tourism industry
- how the image and perception of a destination can impact on its travel and tourism industry
- how to anticipate future trends in the travel and tourism industry.

You could show what you have learned by:

- researching the range of transport available and establishing the most eco-friendly and sustainable form for tourism purposes and how this could be promoted
- using a hypothetical airline with a negative image to identify a marketing strategy that will improve its public perception
- investigating the tourism trends of the future and the future of the travel industry.

Principal learning topics

Principal learning for the Advanced Diploma in Travel and Tourism is delivered via the following eight topics.

People in travel and tourism

This topic includes:

- learning about the different fields and organisations in the sector, its key human resource practices, different management roles and the impact of leadership styles
- an in-depth look at different jobs and their requirements.

Destinations and cultures

This topic includes:

- a look at the key destinations in the UK and worldwide, and developing an understanding of their appeal
- ethical tourism and its benefits.

Environmental influences

This topic includes:

- an understanding of the environmental impacts and pressures of travel, destination developments and visitors
- the costs and benefits of environmentally-friendly practices.

Image and perception

This topic includes:

- understanding how positive and negative images and perceptions are acquired and their impact on destinations, businesses and staff
- the opportunity to plan a promotional campaign and use pricing to influence image and perception.

Political and economic influences

This topic includes:

- learning how political and economic decisions by the UK and other governments affect the UK's travel and tourism sector
- the significance to the sector of global incidents or crises.

Technology in travel and tourism

This topic includes:

- an understanding of the development of technology
- learning about software and developing relevant skills.

Changes and trends

This topic includes:

- learning about what drives change and how this affects the sector's structure, business activities, products and services
- the reasons for changes in popularity, analysing current tendencies and anticipating future trends.

Creating and delivering travel and tourism products and services

This topic includes:

- developing knowledge and employability skills in a real-life scenario, actively dealing with customers and suppliers to create a travel or tourism product or service for target customers.

ASL for the Diploma in Travel and Tourism

Choosing the right ASL is very important, and at each level of the Diploma you will be able to develop your interest in travel and tourism by taking specialist courses relating to your chosen subject and career ambitions. You might take a course in teaching English as a second language or train in customer service. You could also choose a subject such as business studies, geography or economics as an A level to help you get on to a university course. You can also broaden your learning by taking additional subjects that reflect your other interests and career ambitions e.g. a humanities subject, an art and design subject or a science. It can be really useful to study a foreign language as well because of the great opportunities to work abroad in the travel and tourism sector.

Given the importance of ASL and the broad range of choices open to you, you would really benefit from impartial information, advice and guidance from a teacher or tutor. Specialist advice and guidance may be needed to help you to choose the right qualifications, and your school or college will be able to provide access to a Connexions adviser or careers adviser.

What applicants for the Diploma in Travel and Tourism have to say about their choice

'I really don't know what job I want to do in the future, but I have always been interested in travel – when I was younger I wanted to be air cabin crew. I think this course will help me widen my ideas a bit and give me more time to think.'

'I am thinking of doing the Diploma in Travel and Tourism because I loved the taster day we did – it was really practical and that's better for me.'

The Diploma in Travel and Tourism and where it could take you

Progression from the Diploma is wide-ranging because the travel and tourism sector spans a huge range of jobs. If you have the right skills, qualities and qualifications, there are many exciting opportunities for you to choose from. A Diploma in Travel and Tourism will give you the skills you need for either education or employment and is a first step towards a career in the sector.

The scope of jobs available in the travel and tourism sector is huge, and it includes:

- tour manager
- tourist information assistant/manager
- theme park worker
- coach driver
- air cabin crew
- airport staff
- travel agent
- resort representative.

The Diploma in Travel and Tourism could lead you on to a university degree in travel and tourism operations, management, business studies, transport planning, air traffic control, adventure tourism or hospitality.

Alternatively, you might take a job with training or an Apprenticeship as a retail travel consultant, resort representative or call centre team member. Because the Diploma in Travel and Tourism teaches you a combination of subjects, you will gain the valuable skills needed whatever route you choose in education and employment.

Further information

To find out more about the Diploma in Travel and Tourism, speak to your teacher or careers adviser.

You can also find more information about Diplomas on these websites:

- www.direct.gov.uk/diplomas
- www.connexions-direct.com
- www.tandtdiploma.co.uk

To find out where you can study for this Diploma in your area, you can visit http://yp.direct.gov.uk/14-19prospectus

If you would like more information about the travel and tourism sector, you could also refer to the following resources and sources of support.

Title: People1st.co.uk
Overview: This comprehensive website for all 14 industries that make up the hospitality, leisure, travel and tourism sector offers information on three key areas – research, vocational learning and business solutions.
Website: www.people1st.co.uk

Title: World Travel and Tourism Council
Overview: Intelligence about the travel and tourism sector informs learning and provides Labour Market Information that will support you in your learning and progression planning.
Website: www.wttc.org

Title: Institute of Travel and Tourism
Overview: This professional organisation's website offers a good source of information and a dedicated careers/education section.
Website: www.itt.co.uk

Title: biz/ed
Overview: This website looks at a variety of business sectors – click the 'Learning Materials' tab and then follow the link to a section on information specific to travel and tourism. This provides a flavour of the jobs available in the sector.
Website: www.bized.co.uk

Title: Careersbox

Overview: Use this resource to find film clips showing jobs in travel and tourism, such as a travel sales adviser with First Choice.

Website: www.careersbox.co.uk

N.B. You many also want to look at the Further Information section under the Diploma in Hospitality (p82) because some of these links are also relevant to areas of travel and tourism.

PART THREE

END NOTE

CHAPTER FIVE

Are you ready to make your decision?

Why don't you try 'diploma bingo' (see Table 4) to identify how prepared you are to make well-informed decisions about your future and whether a Diploma is right for you?

Table 4
'Diploma bingo.' Tick the squares that you agree with – you're aiming for a full house!

DECISION MAKING	DIPLOMAS	PERSONAL PROBLEMS	CHOICES
I know how to research and make well-informed and realistic decisions about whether to do a Diploma	I am able to do a Diploma in up to 14 different subject areas and I know what is available locally	If I have problems in school or at home I have someone to go to who can help me	I will seek advice and listen to others. However, it will be my own choice if I decide to study for a Diploma
WORK EXPERIENCE	**VOLUNTARY WORK**	**CAREERS ADVICE**	**IMPARTIALITY**
I could get a part-time job while doing a Diploma as I know the experience will be invaluable	I could do voluntary work, while doing a Diploma because it would give me an advantage	If I don't know what I want to do in the future, I could get careers advice to find out more about the range of Diploma courses available	I am aware some information I receive about Diplomas may be biased
FINANCIAL SUPPORT	**EMPLOYABILITY SKILLS**	**FURTHER EDUCATION**	**ASPIRATIONS**
If I need help planning my finances, I know where to go	The Diploma will support me in finding out about the skills and qualities I will need in the workplace	If I am considering going to college or staying on at school, I know where and how to get relevant information	I am encouraged to think big and go for my dreams
HIGHER EDUCATION	**SELF-AWARENESS**	**STEREOTYPES**	**YEAR 9 OPTIONS**
If I want to know about going to university, I know who to speak to about doing the right ASL with my Diploma course	I am aware of the type of person I am and what I enjoy doing – this will help me choose the right Diploma course	I am aware of barriers to employment in certain areas of work and know how to challenge them	I have a wide choice of what to study next and I am aware of all of the opportunities available

CHAPTER SIX

What next?

This chapter will give you some more information about what you could do following your Diploma.

Now you have completed your Diploma course, what next?

Currently, compulsory schooling ends at age 16. However, the government is committed to encouraging young people to stay in education or training for longer.

This will give you the best chance to succeed because:

- young people who stay in education after the age of 16 are more likely to gain higher levels of qualifications than those who do not
- young people with Level 2 qualifications earn more than those without (see box below)
- continuing in learning for longer brings benefits for individuals, the economy and society
- extending your participation in learning, whether education or training, means that at the age of 18 you should have the qualifications and experience to carry on to college, university or training or move into skilled work.

Did you know?

Earning potential as a result of longer participation in learning

By continuing in education post-16, young people significantly improve their life chances, employment opportunities, are likely to have better health and are less likely to commit crimes. Additionally, those who gain five or more good GCSEs or a Level 2 qualification earn on average around £100,000 more over their lifetime than someone who leaves learning with qualifications below Level 2!

There are many opportunities available to you at the end of your Diploma course. If you complete your Foundation or Higher Diploma, you could then:

- study a Higher or Advanced Diploma in the same subject area
- study a Higher or Advanced Diploma in a different subject area

- study general qualifications such as A levels
- take an Apprenticeship – with an entitlement, by 2013, to a place for all suitably qualified 16-year-olds
- apply for a job with training
- take a course at college.

Once you've completed your Advanced Diploma, you could then:

- study for a university degree
- study an Advanced Diploma in a different subject area
- apply for an Apprenticeship
- apply for a job with training
- take a course at college.

If you are not sure what option to choose or need help and support to make a well-informed decision then it might be useful to talk to an expert. Your careers adviser or Connexions adviser can help you make the right choice as they have the specialist training to help you tackle personal and career issues. You could also contact a Connexions Direct adviser online at www.connexions-direct.com or by telephone on 0808 001 3219.

Will a Diploma help me get to college and university?

Yes! The Diploma has been designed to broaden your options, and because universities and colleges were involved in creating the qualification, they have been designed to help you develop the skills and knowledge important in further and higher education. This will give you the core skills you need to succeed on a further or higher education course.

The Higher Diploma will enable you to progress to the Advanced Diploma, which may be available at your own or a local school or college.

All universities have said they will accept an Advanced Diploma (equivalent to 3.5 A levels) for entry on to a degree course if you have taken the relevant ASL. It is therefore very important to contact the university admissions tutor to ask about their specific requirements.

Will a Diploma help me get a job?

Yes! The Diploma was designed to increase the options available to you, including preparation for the world of work. It was developed with the help of employers and so is designed to give you knowledge, skills and experience in a variety of relevant settings. Furthermore, as 50% of the principal learning is applied in context, the Diploma will offer you the strong platform you need to do well in the world of work. Remember that going on to further study such as a Higher or Advanced Diploma will mean you have even more to offer once you start your career, and help you earn more over your lifetime.

Will a Diploma help me get an Apprenticeship?

Yes! The Diploma has been designed to develop your practical skills and applied knowledge. The personal, learning and thinking skills you gain will support both team working and independent study, and this fits well with an Apprenticeship, which is a great way to get on-the-job training and study for a nationally recognised qualification. An Apprenticeship gives you the opportunity to earn while you learn, and there are many Apprenticeships linked closely to Diploma lines of learning e.g. in sport and active leisure, retail business, engineering, travel and construction.

Will a Diploma help me study for A levels?

Yes! The Diplomas combine theoretical study and applied learning, while a Higher Diploma will help you study for A levels if that is the right choice for you. A levels offer considerable flexibility:

- a wide range of subjects to choose from
- the opportunity to study subjects you may not have studied before.

A levels consist of two parts: the AS and **A2**. The advanced subsidiary (AS) is a stand-alone qualification, which can be taken on its own and without progression to the A2 stage. The AS tends to cover less demanding material than the A2.

CHAPTER SEVEN

Further information

A range of resources are available to help you research your Diploma decisions.

Title: Diplomas for 14–19-year-olds
Overview: This website features everything you need to know about Diplomas.
Website: http://yp.direct.gov.uk/diplomas

Title: Connexions Direct: Jobs4u
Overview: A generic information, advice and guidance website with a careers resource section that lets you find out about jobs and entry requirements. It is possible to select an occupational area ('job family') to discover more about different jobs or select a specific job using the A–Z search.
Website: www.connexions-direct.com/jobs4u

Title: National Guidance Research Forum: Labour Market Information Future Trends
Overview: This website offers detailed information on different sectors such as numbers employed, skills shortages, types of role, qualification levels, future trends, regional information and a breakdown of the sector in relation to gender, ethnicity and age profiles.
Website: www.guidance-research.org/future-trends

Title: Apprenticeships: Opening doors to a better future
Overview: This website offers general information together with specific details of all types of Apprenticeship.
Website: www.apprenticeships.org.uk

Title: Prospects
Overview: The UK's official graduate careers website presents detailed information on different career sectors.
Website: www.prospects.ac.uk

Title: UCAS
Overview: The UCAS website gives lots of useful general information about higher education and links to other sources of help e.g. financial support. It is also where learners apply online for higher education courses. The Course Search section is a great way for Diploma students to explore related higher education courses and the relevant entry requirements.
Website: www.ucas.ac.uk

Title: Careersbox
Overview: This resource contains more than 300 searchable video job profiles.
Website: www.careersbox.co.uk

Title: Which Way Now?
Overview: This Connexions site offers information about options at Key Stage 4.
Website: www.connexions-direct.com/whichwaynow

Title: It's Your Choice
Overview: This Connexions site provides progression information about post-16 choices.
Website: www.connexions-direct.com/itsyourchoice

Title: Education Maintenance Allowance
Overview: Information is available here on financial support for post-16 learning.
Website: http://ema.direct.gov.uk

Glossary of terms and initialisations

A level   Advanced level course.

A2   The second half of a full A level.

**Additional and   **ASL includes optional subjects that you can choose when doing
**specialist   **a Diploma. It gives you the opportunity to broaden your studies.
learning (ASL) This part of your learning includes qualifications in specific
occupational areas (specialist learning) or other areas of study
(additional learning) depending on your own individual abilities and
aspirations.
ASL qualifications must be chosen from a list of approved
qualifications available from the National Database of Accredited
Qualifications (www.accreditedqualifications.org.uk) – there is a
wide range of courses to choose from.

Apprenticeship An opportunity for you to earn as you learn, because you get the
chance to train while working in particular skilled areas.

AS level   Advanced subsidiary. It forms the first half of a full A level, but is
also a qualification in its own right.

CV   Curriculum vitae. A summary of your achievements and other
details of your life that relate to an application for a course or
employment.

DCSF   The Department for Children, Schools and Families, which has
now been replaced by the Department for Education.

Diploma   A new qualification to recognise achievement from the ages of
14 to 19, combining practical skill development with theoretical
and technical understanding and knowledge.

Employability skills These are essential skills that are transferable to a variety of
situations and necessary for success in the workplace in the 21st
century e.g. team working, problem solving and communication
skills.

Further education Further education includes courses in a wide range of subjects and
at different levels for those over the compulsory school leaving age.
Qualifications can be taken in their own right or can be used to
meet entry requirements for higher education.

Generic learning This includes the more general skills and knowledge that you
will need in employment. It includes the following components: a
project; functional skills; personal learning and thinking skills; work
experience.

Principal learning

This includes the knowledge, understanding and skills that are specific to a particular subject and are compulsory. It also includes developing an awareness of any current issues related to the subject. Half of the principal learning content must be delivered through work-related learning.

careers UNCOVERED

LIFTING THE LID ON CAREERS

For the full series visit www.trotman.co.uk

Estd.1969 trotman t

Choose the right qualifications

"This will help guide students through one of the toughest decisions they will have to take at school"
www.unilibro.it

- Advice on choosing post–16 options

- Guidance on future career aspirations

- Also includes the new diploma

978 1 84455 163 7

£14.99

Buy your copy today at **www.trotman.co.uk**

 trotman | t

REAL life GUIDES

THE ARMED FORCES
2nd Edition

CREATIVE INDUSTRIES

HOSPITALITY & EVENTS MANAGEMENT

GET A REAL INSIGHT INTO CAREERS

MANUFACTURING & PRODUCT DESIGN

SPORT & ACTIVE LEISURE

CHILDCARE

For the full series visit www.trotman.co.uk

trotman | t

Essential exam tips for every student

"Addresses every exam–related issue"
Career Guidance Today

- Survive exams with confidence

- Tips on how to get organised

- Advice on managing stress levels

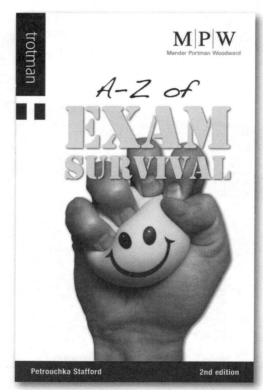

trotman

M|P|W
Mander Portman Woodward

A-Z of

EXAM
SURVIVAL

Petrouchka Stafford   2nd edition

978 1 84455 134 7   £9.99

Buy your copy today at **www.trotman.co.uk**   trotman | t